Supporting English Language Learners in Math Class

Grades 3–5

Rusty Bresser
Kathy Melanese
Christine Sphar

Math Solutions
Sausalito, California, USA

To all English language learners . . .

*We appreciate the linguistic and cultural diversity
that they bring to our classrooms and are grateful
to their teachers for welcoming them
with high expectations and support.*

Math Solutions
150 Gate 5 Road
Sausalito, CA 94965
www.mathsolutions.com

Library of Congress Cataloging-in-Publication Data

Bresser, Rusty.
  Supporting English language learners in math class, grades 3/5 / Rusty Bresser, Kathy Melanese, Christine Sphar.
      p. cm.
  Includes bibliographical references and index.
  ISBN 978-0-941355-85-8 (alk. paper)
  1. Mathematics—Study and teaching (Elementary)   2. English language—Study and teaching (Elementary)—Foreign speakers.   I. Melanese, Kathy.   II. Sphar, Christine.   III. Title.
  QA135.6.B735 2008
  372.7—dc22

                                                                                  2008021358

Editor: Toby Gordon
Production: Melissa L. Inglis-Elliott
Cover design: Jan Streitburger
Interior design: Joni Doherty
Composition: ICC Macmillan Inc.

Printed in the United States of America on acid-free paper
12 11 10   ML   3 4 5

A Message from Math Solutions

We at Math Solutions believe that teaching math well calls for increasing our understanding of the math we teach, seeking deeper insights into how children learn mathematics, and refining our lessons to best promote students' learning.

Math Solutions shares classroom-tested lessons and teaching expertise from our faculty of professional development instructors as well as from other respected math educators. Our publications are part of the nationwide effort we've made since 1984 that now includes

- more than five hundred face-to-face professional development programs each year for teachers and administrators in districts across the country;
- annually publishing professional development books, now totaling more than seventy titles and spanning the teaching of all math topics in kindergarten through grade 8;
- four series of videos for teachers, plus a video for parents, that show math lessons taught in actual classrooms;
- on-site visits to schools to help refine teaching strategies and assess student learning; and
- free online support, including grade-level lessons, book reviews, inservice information, and district feedback, all in our *Math Solutions Online Newsletter*.

For information about all of the products and services we have available, please visit our website at *www.mathsolutions.com*. You can also contact us to discuss math professional development needs by calling (800) 868-9092 or by sending an email to *info@mathsolutions.com*.

We're always eager for your feedback and interested in learning about your particular needs. We look forward to hearing from you.

Contents

Foreword

Writing this book began with our conviction that communication is key to the teaching and learning of mathematics. Communication involves talking, listening, reading, writing, demonstrating, and observing. It means participating in social interaction, sharing thoughts with others, and listening to others share their ideas.

Communication helps children construct understandings of mathematical ideas and develop connections between their informal knowledge and the abstract symbolism of mathematical concepts. Communication makes mathematical thinking observable, thus making mathematical talk critical to the assessment process and to learning itself. Teachers find out what students understand or are confused about by listening to their ideas. And communication encourages students to reflect on their own knowledge and can help them clarify their ideas or change their thinking, especially when they hear others' points of view. Communicating about mathematical ideas is therefore important to both the teacher and the student.

While communication is important to mathematical learning, it can also increase inequity for English language learners (ELLs). If math instruction and modes of communication are in English, students who are English language learners will not have equal access to classroom discussions unless teachers provide extra support. The equity principle in *Principles and Standards for School Mathematics* (NCTM 2000) states that all students, regardless of their personal characteristics, backgrounds, or physical challenges, must have opportunities to study and learn mathematics.

Equity in math instruction does not simply mean that everyone receives the same math lesson. Equity means that English language learners deserve the opportunity to be as successful as their peers who grew up speaking English. For many English language learners, especially those not given a chance to learn in their primary language, the assumption has existed that they will acquire English just through immersion in an English-speaking classroom. Likewise, ELLs are expected to learn math content just by being present for the math lessons. Ignoring the role of student participation and communication in math lessons can lead to inequity in the education of this population.

This is not to say that ELLs aren't as capable as their peers or are somehow lacking in what is needed to achieve in school. Students who speak another language bring a unique linguistic experience with them to school. Many times it is just a language barrier that prevents them from demonstrating the depth of their understanding of the content presented. They are in no way deficient. In fact, the opposite is true. They bring the diverse cultural traditions of their home with them to school and help educate us about acceptance, tolerance, and respect of differences.

The language of instruction is transparent to teachers who are native English speakers. Not so for English language learners. English, as all languages, has a complex structure that native speakers begin learning early in life and later use effortlessly and automatically. Our hope is that with this book, you will see some of the hidden pieces of language that seem so obvious to those of us who speak English as a native language. By providing your students with ongoing explicit language instruction, even during math, you are giving them an opportunity to learn both English and content matter. Language and thought are connected; we can't have one without the other. And thinking is what we hope to facilitate with each math lesson. Therefore, in order to provide an equitable education for our ELLs, we are obligated to recognize their needs and make modifications in our instruction in order to provide the richest experiences in education for all students. Our interest in designing those modifications to support teachers is what led us to write this book.

Working with English learners, while rewarding, is not easy. The fact that teachers conduct their instruction in a language that some students do not yet use fluently forces teachers to rethink the most basic element of their work, the medium of instruction. Many politicians are ready to point fingers at teachers for the gap in achievement between English language learners and their native English-speaking peers. But few of these critics are ready with concrete suggestions as to how to modify the very medium of instruction in order to improve the success of ELLs. As teachers ourselves, we know that time is one of the most valuable commodities in education. Adding a curricular goal, namely English language development, only puts more demands on instructional time. When designing the lesson modifications proposed in this book, we sought to find ways in which content goals and language development goals could be met at the same time. We also held to the philosophy that the best intervention is effective first teaching. By actively involving English language learners in math lessons *and* in language development simultaneously, we increase the learning that takes place in each and every lesson and reduce the amount of time needed to provide individualized or small-group instruction. Language development will always take time; we offer suggestions to make sure it's time well spent.

As teachers, as university faculty, and as instructional coaches, we collaborated over lesson plans, in the classroom, and at the computer to create a resource that would promote communication in the instruction of mathematics, provide equity for students learning in their second language, and support teachers in accomplishing the goals of content instruction and language development.

Acknowledgments

We'd like to thank the following people for making this book possible: Toby Gordon, Joan Carlson, and David Bautista for their editorial expertise; Melissa L. Inglis-Elliott for her work on the book's production; Marilyn Burns for her support; and Susana Dutro and the California Reading and Literature Project for their groundbreaking work with English language learners.

We'd like to thank the following principals and teachers for allowing us to work at their schools and in their classrooms: from Lexington Elementary School, El Cajon, CA: Principal Sylvia Casas-Werkman, Gina García, Kris Candib, Deborah Hunter, and Janet Ilko; from Central Elementary School, National City, CA: Principal Alfonso Denegri, Kathrina Mendoza; from Jackson Elementary School, San Diego, CA: Principal Rupi Boyd, Tina Rasori.

Christine Sphar would like to thank her parents for their support, her husband for his patience, the wonderful children and teachers of Lexington Elementary for their vitality, and her coauthors for their professional curiosity and work ethic.

Rusty Bresser would like to thank his coauthors for their creative collaboration and for sharing their wisdom about English language development. And as always, gracias chivito.

Kathy Melanese would like to thank her parents for their unwavering belief in her ability to accomplish anything she desired; Trevor, Amanda, and Nicholas, who are the light of her life and make her smile every day; her husband, who makes her dreams come true; the amazingly dedicated teachers and students of National City; and finally, her coauthors, who provided an incredible experience in learning and collaboration.

Teaching Math to English Language Learners 1

If you are a classroom teacher, it is likely that you have students in your class for whom English is a second language. It is also likely that, while language arts is their biggest challenge of the school day, these students are struggling in mathematics. Achievement data show that English language learners (ELLs) are not performing at the same levels as their native English-speaking counterparts (NAEP 2007). This inequity can be addressed if teachers provide well-designed extra support for their students.

Why should teachers have to address English language development (ELD) during the precious academic time allotted to the instruction of mathematics? After all, in many schools across the United States, ELD has its own mandated daily instructional minutes. And teachers have learned strategies for helping ELLs understand their lessons. Isn't the incorporation of visuals, the use of manipulatives, and a conscious effort to read word problems aloud enough to address the needs of these students?

English language learners need to learn the content of their mathematics courses. But learning is mediated through language—in our case, the English language. Every part of learning is language dependent, from the arousal of a curiosity, to the teacher's explanation of a concept, to the formation of an understanding of that concept, to the verbalization or written expression of that understanding. Along the path from curiosity to demonstrated understanding, a learner—any learner—needs to clarify his developing understanding, test hypotheses, and solicit confirmation of his thinking. All of these activities are conducted through the medium of language. When a learner is carrying out all of this cognitive work in a second language, limitations in language can lead to limitations in learning. Compounding this situation is the time crunch that faces students of mathematics: each year math becomes more challenging and more abstract.

Therefore, in classrooms where instruction is provided only in English, the more support given to English language learners, the sooner they can enter and appreciate the world of mathematics.

This book is intended to assist teachers in helping their students accomplish two goals: develop their proficiency in English and develop their mathematical understanding. To that end, the lessons in the book seek to amplify rather than simplify the role of language in math class. The lessons show different ways that teachers can explicitly structure experiences so that all students, especially ELLs, can engage in conversations about math in English that promote better understanding of the content being taught.

To accomplish these goals, it is important for teachers to be aware of the factors that contribute to English language learners' success in mathematics. These include the backgrounds and experiences that these students bring to the classroom; how students acquire a second language; the challenges ELLs face when learning mathematics; determining the linguistic demands of a math lesson; and specific strategies and activities that simultaneously support learning English and learning mathematics with understanding.

The Backgrounds of English Language Learners

There are approximately five million ELLs enrolled in public schools in the United States (National Clearinghouse for English Language Acquisition 2007). That's more than 10 percent of the school population. And every year, the percentage of ELLs increases. In some states, ELLs represent a far larger portion of the school population. In California, for example, more than 25 percent of students are English language learners (California Department of Education 2006–2007). Texas, New York, Florida, Illinois, and Arizona also have substantial numbers of students who are learning English as a second language. In some states, the school population of English language learners is relatively not as large, but the percent increase in recent years is significant. In the southern United States, for example, the ELL population in schools has increased more than 400 percent in the last ten years (National Clearinghouse for English Language Acquisition 2007).

The profiles of English learners vary in the length of time they've been in the United States and in the amount of schooling they received in their home country. The educational backgrounds of ELLs range from recent arrivals with little or no schooling, or interrupted schooling in their country of origin, to those who have a high degree of literacy in their native language. And there are those students whose families have been in the United States for one or two generations and have maintained their native language at home but have not yet acquired enough English to be proficient in academic settings.

ELLs are enrolled in different types of programs in school, depending on the resources and philosophies of the state or district they are educated in. Many states offer bilingual education in a student's primary language as well as English. This allows students to continue their conceptual growth and literacy skills in the primary language while adding English. When children are provided an education in their first language, they get two things: academic knowledge and literacy skills. Both the knowledge and the literacy skills students develop in their first language help English language development (ELD) enormously. The knowledge students acquire using their first language makes the input they hear and read in English much more comprehensible. This results in more language acquisition and more learning in general (Krashen and Terrell 1983). Teachers of English to Speakers of Other Languages sees the maintenance and promotion of students' native languages as an important part of effective education for students who are learning English (TESOL 2006).

In locations where bilingual education is unavailable for various reasons (no teachers speak the students' language, district or state policies, parent input), ELLs are placed in English-only classrooms, and in some schools and districts they receive English language development as part of the day. Some districts offer newcomer programs for recent immigrants to help them learn some basic survival English and become acquainted with American culture.

The length of time English language learners have been in the United States, the amount of schooling they have had in their home country, and the kinds of support they have received here in our schools all affect their progress in acquiring English. As well, any instruction, including math, that is delivered in English affects students' English language development.

English Language Development

Considering the importance that acquiring English has on learning in the content areas, ELD instruction should be based on sound theoretical principles of how children acquire a second language. Dutro and

Moran (2003) discuss the differences between the theories of the natural acquisition of English (Krashen and Terrel 1983), which is the idea that language can be acquired in a natural way through meaningful interactions, similar to how we acquire our first language, and the direct instruction of English (McLaughlin 1985). Dutro and Moran argue that there needs to be a balance between the two theories, stating that "a comprehensive theory of classroom instruction should incorporate both informal and formal-language learning opportunities" (228).

Filmore and Snow (2000) echo this idea by explaining that certain conditions must be present for children to be successful in learning English. They state that ELLs must interact directly and frequently with people who are expert speakers of English, which mirrors the natural process of language acquisition; however, if that condition is not met for any reason, then direct instruction in English is essential for language learning. Therefore, regardless of the students' primary language or school experience, they need systematic, direct instruction for learning English, but the instruction needs to be embedded in a natural, meaningful context with many opportunities for practice. The lessons in this book were developed to include both informal and formal language learning opportunities in math class.

Another aspect of instruction for ELLs is that teachers need to use strategies that give students access to the content in mathematics and other curriculum areas and help them learn the sophisticated vocabulary and language structures required in those academic settings. This focus on English as a language, not just as a means of instruction, should cut across all content areas and should be at the forefront of teachers' thinking when planning a lesson. In other words, when we teach math to English language learners, we are also teaching English, not just teaching *in* English. Dutro and Moran (2003) have called this teaching of language prior to content instruction *frontloading*. Dutro, in conjunction with the California Reading and Literature Project (2003), has developed frontloading approaches for language arts curricula in California. We offer here an approach to frontloading English academic language in math.

The Challenges of Teaching Math to English Language Learners

Many educators share the misconception that because it uses symbols, mathematics is not associated with any language or culture and is ideal for facilitating the transition of recent immigrant students into

English instruction (Garrison 1997). To the contrary, language plays an important role in learning mathematics. Teachers use language to explain mathematical concepts and carry out math procedures. While solving problems in mathematics, we often use specialized technical vocabulary (*addition, subtraction, addend, sum*). And researchers of mathematical learning have found that students can deepen their understanding of mathematics by using language to communicate and reflect on their ideas and cement their understandings. Classroom talk can cause misconceptions to surface, helping teachers recognize what students do and do not understand. When students talk about their mathematical thinking, it can help them improve their ability to reason logically (Chapin and Johnson 2006, Cobb et al. 1997, Hiebert and Wearne 1993, Khisty 1995, Lampert 1990, Wood 1999).

The challenge of teaching math to English language learners lies not only in making math lessons comprehensible to students but also in ensuring that students have the language needed to understand instruction and express their grasp of math concepts both orally and with written language. ELLs have the dual task of learning a second language and content simultaneously. For this reason, "it is critical to set both content and language objectives for ELLs. Just as language cannot occur if we only focus on subject matter, content knowledge cannot grow if we only focus on learning the English language" (Hill and Flynn 2006, 22).

ELLs are faced with some common obstacles when learning math. One challenge they face is unknown or misunderstood vocabulary. For example, they can become confused during a discussion if the mathematics vocabulary has different meanings in everyday usage, as with *even, odd,* and *function*. They also may be confused if the same mathematical operation can be signaled with a variety of mathematics terms, such as *add, and, plus, sum,* and *combine*. A word such as *left*—as in "How many are left?"—can be confusing when the directional meaning of the word is most commonly used in everyday English. The words *sum* and *whole* also can cause confusion because they have nonmathematical homophones (*some* and *hole*).

A second obstacle is with an incomplete understanding of syntax and grammar. For example, math questions are often embedded in language that makes the problems unclear or difficult to comprehend. Consider the following problem:

> *Samuel bought 3 bags of oranges with 7 oranges in each bag.*
> *How many oranges did he buy?*

This word problem uses both the past and present tense of the irregular verb *to buy* in one question, which may cause difficulty for an English language learner, depending on the student's English language proficiency.

Consider another problem:

Lisa gave a total of 12 treats to her cats.
She gave her large cat 2 more treats than she gave her small cat.
How many treats did she give to each cat?

Here, students need to understand or figure out the meanings of words such as *total* and *treats*. They also need to understand words that convey a mathematical relationship such as *more . . . than*. In addition, students need to infer that Lisa has only two cats.

English language learners typically experience difficulty understanding and therefore solving word problems, and this difficulty increases in the later grades of elementary school as the word problems become more linguistically and conceptually complex (Cummins 2004). Difficulty with grammar, syntax, and vocabulary lies in both understanding math instruction and having the ability to engage in discussions about math.

Many teachers use strategies to help students understand the content in their math lessons. Scaffolds for learning may include manipulatives, visuals, and graphics. These supports are all essential for building a cursory understanding of math concepts, but they may not provide students enough linguistic support for them to discuss their thinking, which would lead to a deeper understanding of content. For example, let's say that a student's understanding of polygons is based on a two-column chart with drawings that distinguish polygons from shapes that are not polygons. Once the chart is put away, the student may not have internalized enough of the linguistic elements of the lesson to be able to continue her learning in subsequent lessons on polygons. Having the language to talk about math concepts is crucial to developing an understanding of those concepts.

Classroom discussions about math have been shown to deepen students' conceptual understanding. These discussions are a critical aspect of the development of language and content, providing a setting for ELLs to negotiate meaning in daily instructional interactions (García 2003). However, if the language needed to engage in these discussions is not made explicit, ELLs are less likely to benefit from mathematical discussions and can fall further behind their peers.

The challenge for teachers is to focus on math concepts *and* the academic language that is specific to mathematics. Teachers must be cognizant of the linguistic demands of their lessons and how they will address those demands explicitly during instruction so that ELLs can fully participate.

Determining the Linguistic Demands of a Math Lesson

Before providing specific support for ELLs in mathematics, we first need to consider the linguistic demands of a math lesson. This involves determining what academic language students will need to understand and use and knowing how much of the English language students are capable of understanding and producing.

Social or conversational language is the language that students use in familiar, face-to-face situations. This is different than academic language, which includes knowledge of technical and less frequently used vocabulary and ways of speaking English that are not usually heard or used in everyday conversation. The academic language of mathematics includes specialized vocabulary (*polygon, sides, vertices, corners, open, closed, straight, curved*) and the language structures and grammar needed to use the vocabulary (*The* shape *is not a* polygon *because it has* curved sides *and it is* open.).

The publishers of math textbooks often make note of the academic vocabulary being introduced in a particular lesson. Frequently, however, there is no direction provided, either to the teacher or to the students, on how to correctly use the new terms. Just because an English learner is told the meaning of a new word does not mean he can construct a coherent sentence (thought) using that term. Simply knowing the term does not allow the learner to use it to express or develop understanding or learning related to the concept. For example, an English learner might be taught the term *polygon*, but that does not mean the student can draw conclusions, either orally or in writing, about a particular shape and determine whether or not it is a polygon. And if the English learner cannot construct the sentences necessary to talk about particular figures, how will the teacher know what the student has learned?

Once teachers have identified what academic language students will need to know and understand in a particular math lesson, they can then plan strategies for supporting students' ability to use the language in order to carry on mathematical discussions in English. To provide the appropriate support, teachers must be aware that there are varying levels of proficiency with language acquisition.

Given that many teachers have a wide range of levels in their class, from beginning ELLs to fully proficient native English speakers, it can be overwhelming to figure out how to meet all of their needs in one math lesson. It is important, however, for classroom teachers to know each student's level of English proficiency. The descriptions of the levels of English language proficiency differ from state to state. In California, for example, the CELDT (California English Language Development Test) identifies the levels as beginning, early intermediate, intermediate, early advanced, and advanced. In the state of Washington, the levels of English language proficiency are beginning, advanced beginning, intermediate, advanced, and transitional. In Illinois, the levels are described as follows: beginning, developing, expanding, and bridging.

In this book, we identify the English language proficiency levels as beginning, intermediate, and advanced. What's important is that teachers recognize that there *are* different levels of English language proficiency, and that the kind of support they give to students often depends upon how much of the second language students are capable of understanding and producing.

Specific Strategies and Activities That Simultaneously Support Learning English and Learning Math

There are a variety of effective strategies and activities that teachers can use in a lesson that will help all students, particularly English language learners, understand math content and develop English language skills. The use of gestures, manipulatives, charts, and graphs, for example, helps students understand the math content when it is being taught in English. Other strategies and activities, such as the use of sentence frames (e.g., *This is a* _____. *It is/has* _____.) and allowing time for class discussions, provide students with the support and the opportunity to talk about their mathematical ideas in English and actively use the language of mathematics.

While using the following strategies and activities in a math lesson can benefit all students, it is essential for ELLs.

Activate prior knowledge.

Prior knowledge provides the foundation for interpreting new information, and it enables all students, especially English language learners, to make inferences about the meanings of words and expressions that they may not have come across before. The more connections we can make to students' experiences and interests, the more relevance math is likely to assume in students' minds and lives.

Reduce the stress level in the room.

Create a low-stress environment that encourages expression of ideas; where mathematical mistakes are seen as opportunities for learning; and where linguistic mistakes such as incorrect grammar do not inhibit the recognition of good mathematical thinking.

Use sentence frames.

Sentence frames serve a variety of purposes. They provide the support English language learners need in order to fully participate in math discussions; they serve to contextualize and bring meaning to vocabulary; they provide a structure for practicing and extending English language skills; and they help students use the vocabulary they learn in grammatically correct and complete sentences.

After sufficient practice using the frames to express their mathematical thinking, students will be ready to apply the use of the frames for writing.

Create vocabulary banks.

Charts that contain key math vocabulary and phrases are helpful references for ELLs when discussing or writing about their math thinking, especially if the words are accompanied with illustrations.

Practice wait time.

After asking a question, wait for a while before calling on a volunteer. This gives all students, especially English language learners, time to process questions and formulate responses.

Use native language as a resource.

Teachers who know the native language of their students can preview and review vocabulary in the native language. Teachers can also ask students to help others in the class by having them translate, define, and clarify English terms in the students' native language.

In addition, if the students' native language shares cognates with English, these cognates can be pointed out and used to help students understand terms. Cognates are words that share the same ancestral origins and therefore are very similar in two different languages (e.g., *difference* and *diferencia* are English and Spanish cognates). For cognates to be useful, students must know the meanings of the words in their primary language. Lists of cognates are available from a variety of sources. We recommend starting with *The ESL Teacher's Book of Lists* (Kress 1993). The FOSS science series from Britannica (1993) and the CORE *Teaching Reading Sourcebook* (Honig, Diamond, and Gutlohn 2007) are also good resources.

Make manipulative materials available.

Manipulatives serve a variety of purposes and are important tools that can make math content comprehensible to English language learners. Manipulatives give students ways to construct physical models of abstract mathematical ideas; they build students' confidence by giving them a way to test and confirm their reasoning; they are useful tools for solving problems; and they make learning math interesting and enjoyable. Manipulatives can also facilitate effective communication by providing a referent for talking about mathematical ideas (Hiebert et al. 1997).

Ask questions that elicit explanations.

Asking good questions can prompt English language learners to discuss their thinking and elaborate on their ideas. Ask questions that elicit more than a yes-or-no response, such as these:

+ What do you think the answer will be? Why do you think that?
+ What is this problem about?
+ What's the first thing you'll do to solve the problem?

Design questions and prompts for different proficiency levels.

Questioning students lets teachers know what students have learned. Answering questions lets students test, confirm, or modify their own understandings. None of these goals can be met unless the questions are structured in a way that produces a response from the students.

Following are examples of questions and prompts we used to support students at different proficiency levels.

Beginning level
English language learners are not always able to answer the questions posed to them, especially when questions are open-ended. A teacher

can provide support and improve participation of students with lower levels of English proficiency by using a prompt that requires a physical response:

 ✦ Show me the circle.
 ✦ Touch the larger number.

Teachers can also ask a question with a yes-or-no answer:

 ✦ Is one number larger than the other?

When asking short-answer questions, the teacher can build the answer into the question for additional support:

 ✦ Is this a triangle or a circle?
 ✦ Is the line horizontal or vertical?
 ✦ Should we add or subtract?

Intermediate and advanced levels
Students with intermediate and advanced levels of proficiency need less support to understand and respond to questions from the teacher, but carefully crafted questions can improve the quality of both their responses and their English. For example, instead of asking an intermediate-level student, "How did you solve the problem?" you might phrase your question this way: "What did you do first, second, and third to solve the problem?" The second question models the structure of a well-crafted answer: "First, I put the blocks in groups of ten. Second, I counted by tens. Third, I added the ones left over." Compare that with the response more likely from the first question: "I counted them." Students with advanced fluency can respond to even more-open-ended questions and prompts, such as "Describe to me the steps you used to solve the problem and explain how you used them."

Use prompts to support student responses.

Prompts can help English language learners get started when responding to a question:

 ✦ You figured it out by . . .
 ✦ It is a polygon because . . .
 ✦ First you put the hexagon on the table, and then . . .

Provide visuals.

Visuals enable students to see a basic concept much more effectively than if we rely only on words. Among the visuals we can use in presenting math content are pictures and photographs, real objects, graphic organizers, drawings on the overhead projector, and charts.

Pose problems in familiar contexts.

When a problem is embedded in a familiar context, English language learners have an easier time understanding the problem's structure and discussing how to solve it.

Elicit nonverbal responses (e.g., thumbs up or down).

Nonverbal responses help teachers check for understanding without requiring students to produce language. English language learners can participate and show that they understand a concept, or agree or disagree with someone's idea, without having to talk. This is especially important for students whose comprehension of English is more advanced than their ability to speak the language.

Demonstrate and model.

When teachers model their thinking or demonstrate an example of how to do an activity in a clear and explicit manner, it helps English language learners get a picture of what to do.

Use dramatization and gestures.

Supplementing verbal discussion with gestures, pantomime, or dramatization can help English language learners bring meaning to explanations, directions, vocabulary, and word problems.

Modify teacher talk.

Speak slowly and use clear articulation. Reduce the amount of teacher talk and use a variety of words for the same idea. Exaggerate intonation and place more stress on important new concepts or questions.

Recast mathematical ideas and terms.

Mathematics has many linguistic features that can be problematic for English language learners. Use synonyms for mathematical words, such as *subtract*, *take away*, and *minus*. At the same time, be aware that using too many terms simultaneously can confuse ELLs.

Consider language *and* math skills when grouping students.

There are times when grouping students with like abilities in math makes sense, especially when those students are all struggling with the same concept or skill. Most of the time, however, students benefit from working in groups where students have varying skill levels in mathematics.

Students also benefit from working in groups where students have different levels of English language competence. However, it is important for teachers to monitor student talk to ensure that all students have the opportunity to engage in mathematical conversations.

Facilitate whole-class discussions.

In a whole-class discussion, the teacher is not engaged in delivering information or quizzing. Rather, she is attempting to give students the chance to engage in sustained reasoning. The teacher facilitates and guides, and the focus is on students' thinking (Chapin, O'Connor, and Anderson 2003).

Allow for small-group discussions.

In a small-group discussion, the teacher typically gives students a question to talk about among themselves, in groups of three to six. The teacher circulates, listening in on discussions, asking questions, and assisting when necessary.

Utilize partner talk.

In partner talk, the teacher asks a question and then gives students a minute or two to put their thoughts into words with their nearest neighbor. Partner talk allows more students to participate in classroom discussions.

Ask for choral responses from students.

When teachers have students echo back a word or phrase, it exposes students to new vocabulary and serves as a model for correct pronunciation, syntax, and grammar.

Rephrase strategies and ideas.

Rephrasing is when the teacher or a student explains a strategy or an idea, in English, that someone else in the group has shared. Rephrasing gives English language learners another opportunity to make sense of an idea. When students rephrase another student's idea or strategy, it helps clarify their thinking and cement their understanding.

Connect symbols with words.

When strategies for solving problems are described, write the number sentences on the board and point to the symbols (such as +, ×, and =), stressing the words in English.

Putting It All Together: How This Book Is Organized

The lessons in *Supporting English Language Learners in Math Class* are designed to help students understand math content and develop their English language skills. While the lessons span the math curriculum, the book isn't intended to provide all the needed lessons for English language learners. Rather, the lessons are meant to serve as examples of how best to provide the necessary support these students require.

Topics for lessons in the book include geometry, arithmetic word problems, data analysis and probability, algebra, and measurement. The lessons were taught to students from a variety of ethnic and socioeconomic backgrounds, whose native languages include English, Spanish, Vietnamese, Chinese, Cambodian, Farsi, Tagalog, Russian, Kurdish, and Arabic.

Each math lesson is preceded by a minilesson that explicitly introduces and teaches the academic language that students will need to understand and use during the actual math lesson. In the minilesson, sentence frames are introduced. The sentence frames are crucial and serve a variety of purposes. Sentence frames provide the support ELLs need in order to fully participate in math discussions; they serve to contextualize and bring meaning to the vocabulary; they provide a structure for practicing and extending English language skills; they help students use the vocabulary they learn in grammatically correct and complete sentences; and they allow for differentiated instruction because they are designed for different levels of English language proficiency. For example, the following frames support students at various language levels in their discussions about polygons:

Beginning

This is a _____. It is/has _____.

This is not a _____. It is/has _____.

Intermediate

> This is a _____ because _____.

> This is not a _____ because _____.

Advanced

> This shape has _____, _____, and
> _____.

> This shape has _____, _____, and
> _____; therefore, it is a polygon.

Following the minilesson, the actual math lesson begins. Now, the ELLs in the class have the support they need to fully participate in class discussions, using language to develop their understanding of math content.

Throughout the lessons, students practice using different language functions, depending on the mathematics that is being taught and the sentence frames used. For example, the following sentence frame helps students describe nouns, such as polygons:

> This is a _____. It is/has _____.

This sentence frame helps students compare and contrast:

> A _____ has _____, but a _____
> has _____.

Other frames assist students in describing a sequence of events:

> First, _____.

> Next, _____.

> Then, _____.

After that, _____.

Finally, _____.

Other frames help students make predictions:

I predict that _____ because _____.

The lessons in this book help students learn to use a variety of language functions while discussing their mathematical ideas in English. These functions include describing nouns, comparing and contrasting, sequencing, describing location, hypothesizing, categorizing, explaining cause and effect, predicting, giving and following directions, making inferences, drawing conclusions, and summarizing.

Each lesson in the book contains the following:

+ an overview that gives a concise summary of the lesson: what students will be doing and learning
+ a math goal and a language goal
+ key vocabulary words
+ a materials list
+ a variety of sentence frames for different language levels to support language production
+ a class profile that provides information regarding the English language proficiency levels of the students in the vignette
+ a vignette from the classroom that has two parts: the first part introduces academic language and sentence frames to support language production, and the second part focuses on the actual math lesson; during each vignette, specific strategies for supporting English language learners are described
+ student work samples
+ step-by-step directions for teaching the lesson

In addition to the sample lessons, we've included a chapter titled "Helping English Language Learners Make Sense of Math Word Problems." Because word problems can be so difficult for English learners to read and understand, and therefore solve, we've provided detailed examples of strategies that teachers can use to help English learners navigate word problems while developing their English language skills.

We've also included a chapter on how to modify math lessons to support English learners. Here, we describe our thinking and planning behind each lesson: how we identified the language demands and developed the sentence frames, and why we chose particular instructional strategies.

And finally, in Chapter 11, "Frequently Asked Questions," we address teachers' concerns and key questions about supporting English language learners in math class.

Meeting the Challenge

Mathematics is the gatekeeper to higher education. In fact, the more mathematics that students take in middle school and high school, the more likely they are to go on to college (U.S. Department of Education 2000). Because English language learners are not achieving at the same levels in math as their native English-speaking counterparts, many are at risk of having the gate to higher education closed to them. Fortunately, teachers *can* make a difference and address this inequity by providing well-designed support so that English learners can develop proficiency in English *and* develop their mathematical understanding.

The prospect of leveling the playing field so that all students have equal access to the math content being taught is exciting yet challenging. Meeting this challenge will require extra support, the kind of assistance that this book describes. It is our hope that teachers view the lessons in *Supporting English Language Learners in Math Class* as models and apply the strategies to their own experiences as they help *all* of their students succeed in mathematics.

2 Identifying and Describing Polygons

A Geometry Lesson

Overview

In this lesson, students learn to identify and describe polygons and compare and contrast them with figures that are not polygons.

Prior to the lesson, students are introduced to vocabulary words that they will need to use as they learn about polygons. Students are taught various sentence frames and use the vocabulary introduced to describe everyday objects in the room.

During the geometry lesson, students use the vocabulary and the sentence frames to describe and compare and contrast shapes. They sort cards containing illustrations of shapes into two groups, polygons and nonpolygons. Finally, each student draws a picture of a polygon and describes what he knows about polygons in writing.

Math Goal: Students will identify and describe the features of polygons and figures that are not polygons.

Language Goal: Students will develop the academic language necessary to describe polygons and figures that are not polygons.

Key Vocabulary: closed, connect, curved, intersect, line segment, open, polygon, sides, straight, vertex, and vertices

Materials

✦ 12 word cards for key vocabulary terms
✦ 6 sentence strips or pieces of construction paper for sentence frames
✦ large two-column chart with drawings of figures that are polygons and figures that are not polygons
✦ *Identifying and Describing Polygons* cards, 1 set of 16 per pair of students (see Blackline Masters)

- ✦ envelopes for holding cards, 1 per pair of students
- ✦ 1 set of enlarged *Identifying and Describing Polygons* cards
- ✦ optional: pocket chart

Sentence Frames That Help Students Describe Polygons and Nonpolygons

Beginning

> *This is a _____ . It is/has_____ .*

> *This is not a _____ . It is/has_____ .*

Intermediate

> *This is a _____ because _____ .*

> *This is not a _____ because _____ .*

Advanced

> *This shape has _____, _____, and _____ .*

> *This shape has _____, _____, and _____ ;*
> *therefore, it is a polygon.*

Class Profile

Of the thirty students in Ms. Handel's class, half are native English speakers, and the other half of the class is made up of beginning, intermediate, and advanced English speakers.

From the Classroom ✦ **Identifying and Describing Polygons**

Minilesson Introducing Academic Language

Christine Sphar greeted the students in Ms. Handel's class and told them that they would be learning about geometry.

"I have some cards with words written on them," she said, "and the first thing we're going to do is learn what the words mean and practice using them in complete sentences." To help make communication comprehensible to the English learners in the class, Christine enunciated her words clearly and spoke at a slightly slower pace than she would normally speak.

To begin, Christine placed the word *curved* into a large pocket chart at the front of the room. As she put the card in the chart, she read the word aloud to the class. To activate students' prior knowledge, she asked if anyone knew what the word *curved* meant.

"It's like folded," Juan said. "It's like wobbly."

"It's like on the letter S, it's curved," Juliana described.

Christine held up a quarter, running her index finger around its curved side and said, "This is curved."

Christine directed the class to say the word *curved* aloud together in a choral voice. Then she asked the students to find something in the room that was curved. Students identified several objects in the room, including a classmate's curly hair, a coiled cord, and the clock. Each time someone found something that was curved, Christine ran her fingers along the object's curves, providing visual clues.

Next, Christine introduced the word *straight* and placed the word card into the pocket chart. She held up a ruler and ran her finger up and down and said, "This is straight." Again, she had the class read the word aloud, asked for the word's meaning, and directed students to find things in the room that were straight.

"The border of the bulletin board has straight and curved lines!" Joan exclaimed.

"That thing that holds the flag is straight," Abraham said.

"The flag holder is straight," Christine said, adding a new word to Abraham's developing vocabulary in English.

Cindy, whose English language skills are further developed than Abraham's, added, "The edge of the desk is straight."

To help all the students make sense of the word *straight*, Christine had them each touch the edge of their desk and say the word aloud together.

Continuing, Christine introduced the word *line segment* by asking the students to each make a line by stretching their arms out in either direction.

"A line goes on forever in both directions," Christine explained. "A line segment is part of a line."

Christine held up a book, illustrating that each side, or line segment, of the book had two end points. Next, she used a yardstick to point out line segments on the ceiling panels, showing students where each line segment began and ended. Then she asked students to find examples of line segments in the room.

Before moving on, Christine pointed out to the students that the word *segment* in English is similar to the word *segmento* in Spanish. Cognates, or words that sound similar and have the same meaning in two languages, can be helpful to English learners if the students' native language is one that shares cognates with English.

Christine next introduced the word *sides* to the students by drawing different geometric figures on the board (e.g., a square and a triangle) and asking how many sides each figure had. As she pointed to the sides on each shape, Christine introduced the words *vertex* and *vertices*, pointing to the places on the shapes where the sides or line segments connected. Christine used the familiar word *corner* in conjunction with the new word *vertex* to assist the students in their comprehension.

Connect and *intersect* were the next words Christine presented. Once again, she used a strategy called Total Physical Response, asking the students to use both their arms and hands and touch them together to illustrate the word *connect*. She asked students to cross their arms and hands to show the word *intersect*.

In addition, Christine drew figures on the board and asked students to say whether the sides or line segments connected or intersected.

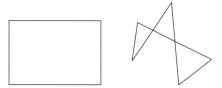

Finally, Christine introduced the words *closed* and *open* in the same manner: drawing figures on the board and asking students to say whether each figure was closed or open.

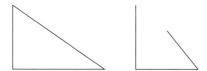

"If a dog is in a *closed* shape, like a fenced-in yard, he can't get out," Christine said. "But the dog can get out if the shape or figure is *open.*" Making connections to real-life situations can help English learners make sense of the new words they are learning.

When Christine finished introducing the vocabulary students would need for the upcoming lesson on polygons, the pocket chart at the front of the room was filled with the following word cards, each of which included a small illustration that provided a clue to the word's meaning. These visual clues are important to English learners because they provide support for comprehending vocabulary words.

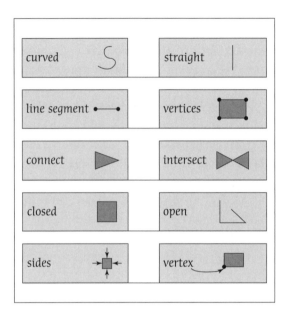

Introducing Sentence Frames

Learning new vocabulary is not the only language demand that will be placed on students during this lesson. Students will also need to be able to use the vocabulary in complete sentences in English. To help students express their understanding of polygons, Christine introduced several sentence frames intended to support students with varying levels of linguistic competence in English: beginning, intermediate, and advanced.

To prepare for this part of the lesson, Christine had sentence frames written on tag board sentence strips. To begin, she placed the first frame in the pocket chart at the front of the room:

This is a _____ . *It is/has* _____ .

Christine started by having the students read aloud the frame, pausing for the blank spaces. Then she modeled for the students how to use the sentence frame. She purposely incorporated the new vocabulary in the pocket chart as well as familiar objects in the classroom.

Pointing to the rim of the clock on the wall, she said, "This is a clock. It is curved."

"Did you notice that I used the vocabulary words in the pocket chart in my sentence?" Christine pointed out.

She modeled another example, pointing to the vent in the wall. "This is a vent. It has four sides." When she was finished with her sentence, she directed the class to repeat it in a choral voice for practice.

Christine then gave the students some think time before practicing the sentence frames with a partner. Think time is crucial, in part because producing language is typically more difficult than comprehending it. Students need time to think about how they'll construct their sentences in English.

After giving students a few seconds to think, Christine directed them to turn to a partner and practice. Following is an exchange between Abraham, who is an intermediate-level English learner, and Joan, who is at an advanced level.

Abraham: This is a table. It is square.

Joan: This is a table. It has four sides.

Here is an exchange between Steph, who is an intermediate-level English learner, and Gina, who is a beginning English speaker.

Steph: This is a book. It has four sides.

Gina: This is a calendar. It has four shapes.

As partners practiced, Christine circulated around the room, monitoring students. As she listened in, she noticed that some students, like Joan, were using the vocabulary in the pocket chart in their sentences, while other students, such as Abraham, were using correct sentences but not including the new vocabulary. And there were a few students, like Gina, who had the right idea, but used some incorrect words, like *shapes* when she meant *sides*.

When the students were finished, Christine called them back to attention and asked Ruth to share her sentence.

Identifying and Describing Polygons

"This is a rectangle. It has four squares," Ruth said.

"This is a rectangle. It has four . . . ," Christine repeated, prompting Ruth to use the correct word by pointing to the sides of a rectangle she quickly drew on the board.

Ruth caught on, and repeated, "This is a rectangle. It has four sides."

"Ruth used one of the words in the pocket chart," Christine told the class.

Cindy went next. She pointed to the globe and said, "This is a sphere. It has no sides."

Dan, an advanced English speaker, added, "This is a rectangle. It is a closed shape."

Carmen, a beginning English speaker, said, "This is door."

There was a long pause. Then she added, "It has four . . ."

After another long pause, Carmen looked to the pocket chart for help and found the word she was looking for. "This is a door. It has four sides," she said.

"One more example," Christine urged the class.

"This is a door. It has four angles," Dan said.

Next, Christine placed a new sentence frame in the pocket chart, one that was a bit more difficult than the first. As with the first frame, she directed the class to read it together, pausing for the blank spaces:

This is a _____ because _____.

"How is this frame different than the first?" Christine asked the class. "What word did I add?"

"It's almost the same, but you added *because*," Juliana noted.

Christine then modeled the new sentence frame by saying, "This [*pointing to the ceiling panel*] is a rectangle because the opposite sides are the same length."

Christine gave students some think time before practicing the sentence frame with a partner. Partner talk is essential for English learners because it gives all students a chance to practice their English language skills.

Following is an exchange between Amanda, a beginning English speaker who recently immigrated from Mexico, and Julio, an intermediate English speaker.

Julio: This is a triangle because it has three sides and three angles.

Amanda: This is square [*long pause; she looks at pocket chart for a sentence frame and decides to use the first one, which is easier*]. This is square. It has four sides.

Julio: This is an octagon [*pointing to a picture of an octagon on a chart in the room*] because it has eight sides.

After partners had practiced, Christine introduced a third sentence frame. This frame was intended for advanced English speakers, but it could be used by any student in the class. Like the other frames, Christine directed the class to read the frame aloud together:

> *This shape has _____, _____, and _____.*

She then modeled how to use the frame. "OK, I'm going to look at the clock," she said, pointing to it. "This shape has a curve, no vertices, and it is closed."

Christine then held up a piece of paper and asked the students to think about how to describe it using the new frame. She gave students time to think, then called on Abraham.

He began, "This shape has four sides, connect lines . . ." Abraham paused for a long time before Christine jumped in to give him support.

"Connecting lines, and . . . ," she prompted.

Abraham continued, "This shape has four sides, connecting lines, and it's open. I mean it's closed."

When Abraham finished his sentence, Christine took a picture frame from Ms. Handel's desk and held it up.

"What can you say about this shape?' she asked the class. "Talk with a partner and try to use one of the sentence frames in the pocket chart."

As Christine circulated around the room, she noticed that students were using the sentence frames that were most appropriate for their language level. For example, rather than using the most complex frame that was just introduced, Carmen, a beginning English speaker, chose to use an easier sentence frame. "This is a rectangle because it has four sides," Carmen said to her partner.

Identifying and Describing Polygons

Introducing the Lesson

For the polygon lesson, Christine had prepared a piece of paper with a two-column chart on which she had drawn figures that were polygons on one side and figures that were not polygons on the other side:

Polygons	Not polygons

After taping the chart to the board and placing the *polygons* word card in the pocket chart, Christine asked the students what they noticed about the figures that were polygons. Before eliciting student ideas, Christine had the students practice saying the word *polygon* several times.

"They're closed," Steph observed.

"They're different shapes," Dan said.

"All the sides are touching," Juliana added.

"What word can we use besides *touching*?" Christine asked, attempting to get the students to use the vocabulary words they'd been introduced to.

"The sides of the polygons are all connected," Julio said.

Christine wrote Julio's sentence on the board and directed the class to read it aloud together. Always thinking of ways to focus on language during a math lesson, Christine asked, "Which adjective describes the sides of the polygon?"

To give the students a clue, Christine held up the word cards *straight* and *curved* from the pocket chart.

"Straight!" the class responded.

"What do you notice about the figures that are not polygons?" Christine asked.

"The polygons," Amanda began, then she paused and corrected herself, "those ones that are not polygons are open."

"They're open and curved," Cindy said.

"They are not connected," Diana said.

"That shape is intersect," Julio said, as he walked up to the board and pointed to this shape:

"It has intersecting lines," Christine added. She was careful to accept Julio's attempt, yet she also knows that explicitly modeling correct usage can further students' English language development.

After students had finished making observations about the figures on the chart, Christine added two more sentence frames to the pocket chart:

This is not a _____. It is/has _____.

This is not a _____ because _____.

"You can use these two sentence frames to describe shapes that are not polygons," Christine said. "Who would like to give us some examples using the sentence frames?"

Juliana pointed to the same shape that Julio had pointed to on the two-column chart:

"This is not a polygon. It has intersecting lines," she said. Then, pointing to the same shape, she continued, "This is not a polygon because it has intersecting lines."

"The sentence frames are almost the same," Christine commented.

Then Christine added onto the third sentence frame she had intro-duced earlier. She wrote on the board:

Then she drew a rectangle on the board that looked like this:

"Who can use the new sentence frame to describe this polygon?" Christine asked the class.

Cindy gave it a try. "This shape has four angles, straight sides, and no curved lines; therefore, it is a polygon." Cindy is an example of how students who are advanced English speakers can serve as good models for the rest of the class.

Next, Christine drew figures on the board, one at a time, and asked students to give a thumbs-up if the figure was a polygon and a thumbs-down if it was not a polygon. Asking English learners to participate in this nonverbal fashion is effective because it is nonthreatening, involves everyone at once, and allows students to develop their understanding without having to produce any language.

"What about this one?" Christine asked as she drew this figure on the board:

Most students' thumbs were turned down. Christine asked if any-one could explain why he or she thought the figure wasn't a polygon.

"It is not a polygon. It is curved," Joan said, using the sentence frame on the pocket chart as a support.

"But it's closed," Abraham said, with a confused tone to his voice.

"You're right, Abraham," Christine acknowledged. "Figures that are not polygons can be closed. But if a figure is closed and it has curves, it isn't a polygon, right?"

Students nodded their heads in agreement.

Next, Christine drew this shape on the board:

"What do you think?" Christine asked. "Thumbs up if it's a polygon and thumbs down if it isn't."

When most students had their thumbs up, Christine called on Amy.

"This is a polygon because it has straight lines and it's closed," Amy said.

After Amy finished, Christine drew this figure on the board:

This time, Christine waited for about ten seconds before she called on someone to explain why the shape was not a polygon. Using wait time is crucial for English learners because it gives them time to formulate their ideas. The longer Christine waited, the more hands shot up in the air. Finally, she called on Franco, a beginning English speaker.

"This is not a polygon. It is open," he said, using one of the most basic sentence frames from the pocket chart.

Sorting Polygons and Nonpolygons

To give students time to identify and describe polygons with a partner, Christine handed out an envelope to each pair of students. Inside each envelope were sixteen cards; on each card there was a figure that was either a polygon or not a polygon. Christine explained to the students that they were to take the cards from the envelope and sort them into two groups—polygons and not polygons—and talk about why each figure belonged in a chosen group. She encouraged students to use the vocabulary and the sentence frames in the pocket chart to help them in their discussions.

Partners immediately got to work, sorting the cards and comparing and contrasting the figures. During a lesson, and especially while students are engaged in partner talk, Christine tries to check in with a variety of students to ask questions that will extend their mathematical thinking and encourage the use of academic language.

Following is an exchange between Christine and two students: Julio, an intermediate English speaker, and his partner, Maria, a beginning English speaker. The two students were looking at a card with a triangle on it and talking about whether it should go in the polygon group or the other group.

Julio: It's a polygon because it is open.

Christine: Are you sure?

Julio: Oh, because it's closed.

Christine: Are you sure? How do you know?

Julio: The line segments touch [*pointing to the vertices on the triangle*].

Christine: What word could we use to say that?

Julio: [*Looking at the pocket chart*] Connect? The line segments connect.

Christine: Maria, show me lines that connect using your arms.

Maria: [*Uses her arms to act out the term* connect] Connect.

Christine: So is the figure a polygon or not?

Maria: It is a polygon. It is closed.

Julio: And it has connecting lines.

When partners had finished sorting the cards, Christine called them back to attention. In her hand she held a set of cards that were enlarged duplicates of the cards that the students had used for sorting. "I'm going to hold up one of the cards and I want you to tell me whether the figure on the card is a polygon or not a polygon and explain why," Christine instructed.

As she held up one card at a time, the students were given one more opportunity to think about the features of polygons and describe their characteristics using the vocabulary and the sentence frames in the pocket chart.

Writing About Polygons

To provide further practice with describing polygons, Christine distributed a piece of paper to each student and asked the children to draw a polygon and write everything they knew about polygons. She encouraged students to use the vocabulary and sentence frames in the pocket chart to help them. Once students had completed their work, Christine directed them to read their papers to their table partners.

Using a variety of sentence frames can differentiate instruction and meet the needs of students with different levels of linguistic competence. Allowing students to choose which sentence frames to use lets them self-regulate, selecting frames that are appropriate for their language level. Sometimes students stretch their capabilities and further their English language skills by using frames that are challenging for their language level. Carolina, a beginning English speaker, used two different sentence frames to support her writing—one frame at the intermediate level and another frame for advanced English speakers. (See Figure 2–1.)

Juliana, an early advanced English speaker, compared the features of shapes that are polygons with those that are not polygons. (See Figure 2–2.)

You do not have to require students to use the sentence frames. However, when students stray from using the frames, they sometimes struggle with correct usage of English syntax and grammar. Abraham,

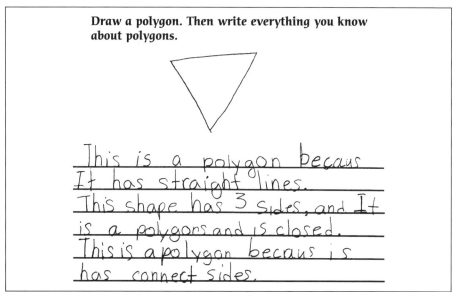

Draw a polygon. Then write everything you know about polygons.

This is a polygon becaus It has straight lines. This shape has 3 sides, and It is a polygons and is closed. This is a polygon becaus is has connect sides.

FIGURE 2-1. Carolina used two sentence frames to support her writing.

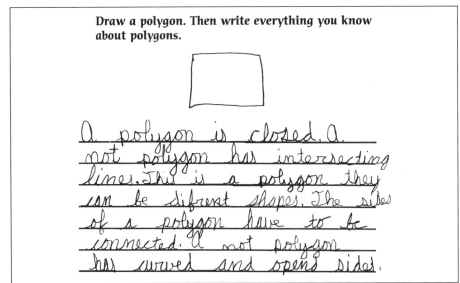

Draw a polygon. Then write everything you know about polygons.

A polygon is closed. A not polygon has intersecting lines. This is a polygon they can be difrent shapes. The sides of a polygon have to be connected. A not polygon has curved and opens sides.

FIGURE 2-2. Juliana compared polygons and nonpolygons.

Draw a polygon. Then write everything you know about polygons.

Polygons is a tipe of shape that are close. The polygons cant have intersect lines. The polygons have straigth lines. A curved shape it is not a polygon. The not polygons don't tuch and they are closed.

FIGURE 2-3. Abraham used key vocabulary to describe polygons.

an intermediate English speaker, demonstrated an understanding of polygons and used important key vocabulary words (*curved, intersect, closed, lines*) to describe them; however, he used incorrect grammar and syntax. (See Figure 2–3.) While using oral or written language can help deepen students' understanding of mathematics, it also provides important practice as they develop grammatical correctness.

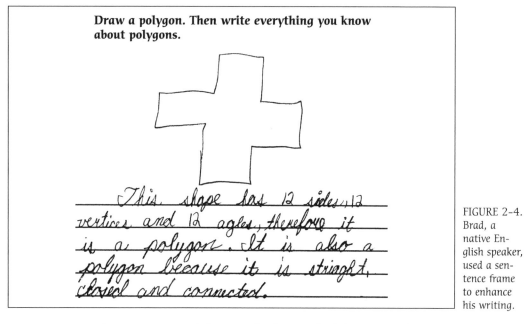

Draw a polygon. Then write everything you know about polygons.

This shape has 12 sides, 12 vertices and 12 angles, therefore it is a polygon. It is also a polygon because it is straight, closed and connected.

FIGURE 2–4. Brad, a native English speaker, used a sentence frame to enhance his writing.

Sentence frames are useful not only for English language learners but also for native English speakers. For example, Brad used one of the frames to enhance his writing. (See Figure 2–4.)

Extending the Lesson

Ms. Handel used sentence frames throughout her unit on geometry. In a lesson she taught several days later, Ms. Handel introduced the following frames to help her students compare and contrast different pairs of polygons, such as a pentagon and a square; a triangle and a trapezoid; a rectangle and a hexagon; and so on.

Sentence Frames That Help Students Compare and Contrast Polygons

Beginning

A _____ has _____.
A _____ has _____.

Intermediate

A _____ has _____, but a _____ has _____.

Advanced

> *While a* _____ *and a* _____ *both have* _____ *,*

> *A* _____ *'s* _____ *are always* _____ *,*
> *but a* _____ *'s* _____ *may not always be* _____ *.*

Activity Directions ✦ **Identifying and Describing Polygons**

Minilesson Introducing Academic Language

1. Using all of the vocabulary words except *polygon*, introduce the word cards, one at a time, and either place them in a pocket chart or tape them to the board. Present an item in the classroom to define and provide a model for each word. For example, show how a circle has curved sides or a table has straight sides. Have the students do hand movements to represent the meaning of the words as well. After modeling each word, direct students to find examples of the word in the classroom (e.g., a clock has curves) and share them with the class.

2. After you have presented all the vocabulary words, introduce the sentence frames, one at a time, using the vocabulary as meaningful practice. Examples:

- ✦ This is a ruler. It is straight.
- ✦ This is a book. It is a closed shape.
- ✦ This is a circle. It is a closed shape.
- ✦ This is a rectangle because it has two sets of equal sides.
- ✦ This shape has a curve, no vertices, and it is closed.

Model first, have the students repeat, and then have students practice in pairs. The partner practice is designed to allow students to use the sentence frames that are most comfortable for them. Each partner should produce three to four sentences before moving on to the next part of the lesson.

The Polygon Lesson

This is the part of the lesson where students are introduced to the math concept of polygons. They will be required to demonstrate their understanding of polygons using the vocabulary and sentence structures provided. This does not preclude students from using other language to express their ability to describe polygons; rather, the frames are intended as a scaffold for students to increase their language production.

1. Present a two-column chart to the students similar to this one:

Polygons	Not polygons
□	⌒⌒
◇	✗
△	⟋⟍
⬠	◗

Remind students of the vocabulary words in the pocket chart that have been introduced and ask them what they notice about the figures underneath the word *Polygons* on your two-column chart. Prompt them to use the vocabulary and sentence frames as support. Practice using the sentence frames to express what the students are describing about polygons. Model, then have the students repeat.

2. Repeat the same procedure with the figures that are not polygons.

3. Draw some figures on the board and ask students whether the figures are polygons or not. Elicit nonverbal responses from students

Identifying and Describing Polygons

(a thumbs-up or a thumbs-down). Ask students in pairs to explain why a figure is or is not a polygon using the sentence frames. Refer to the word chart and sentence frames for language support. Have a few students share their responses orally with the entire class.

4. Distribute an envelope with a set of *Identifying and Describing Polygons* cards to each pair of students. Ask partners to sort the cards into two groups: polygons and not polygons. Direct partners to describe the figures as they sort the cards. Encourage the use of the sentence frames and vocabulary to practice academic language.

5. Show the class an enlarged set of cards. Hold up one card at a time and have students explain whether the figure on the card is or is not a polygon.

6. Direct students to draw a polygon on a piece of paper. Have them explain in writing their understanding of polygons. The word chart and sentence frames will support students in their ability to express their understanding. Have students share their work with a partner.

Build a Shape, Part 1 3

A Geometry Lesson

Overview

In this two-part lesson, students build a shape from pattern blocks that is hidden from the view of their partner. Then, using location words (prepositions), the builder describes to her partner where to put his blocks so that he can create the exact same shape.

Math Goal: Students will describe location and movement using common language and geometric language.

Language Goal: Students will be able to use prepositions to describe the location of specific geometric shapes (or pattern blocks).

Key Vocabulary: above, below, hexagon, on, rhombus, sides, square, to the left of, to the right of, trapezoid, triangle, vertex, vertices

Materials

- pattern blocks, at least 1 of each block (hexagon, trapezoid, triangle, square, blue rhombus, and tan rhombus) per student
- small zip-top bags to hold pattern blocks, 1 per student
- 1 set of overhead pattern blocks
- 13 word cards for key vocabulary terms
- 5 sentence strips or pieces of construction paper for sentence frames
- file folders, 1 per pair of students
- optional: pocket chart

Sentence Frames That Help Students Describe Polygons

Beginning

> This is a _____. It is/has _____.

Intermediate and Advanced

> This is a _____ because _____.

Sentence Frames That Help Students Describe the Location of the Pattern Blocks

All Students

> Put the _____ on the _____.
> above
> below
> to the right of
> to the left of

Beginning

> The _____ should touch.

Intermediate and Advanced

> The _____ of the _____ should touch the _____ of the _____.

Class Profile

Of the thirty students in Ms. Handel's class, half are native English speakers, and the other half of the class is made up of beginning, intermediate, and advanced English speakers.

From the Classroom ✦ **Build a Shape**

Minilesson Introducing Academic Language

Before she began the lesson, Christine Sphar distributed to each pair of students a small plastic zip-top bag full of pattern blocks. To give the students some time to acquaint themselves with the materials, Christine had them explore the blocks for a few minutes before beginning the minilesson. This way, the students would be less apt to play with the pattern blocks once the lesson got under way. When the exploration time was over, Christine addressed the class.

"Today we're going to play a game using the pattern blocks you just received," Christine told Ms. Handel's students. She continued, "You're going to work with a partner and build something with the blocks that your partner can't see. Then you're going to describe what you built so that your partner will be able to build the exact same thing without looking at your blocks."

The students seemed excited about the idea of playing a math game. Games can provide excellent contexts for involving English language learners in conversations about mathematics.

"But first, I'm going to introduce some words you'll need to know and use while you're playing *Build a Shape,*" Christine told the class.

She took an orange square from her bag of transparent pattern blocks and placed it onto the overhead projector. To activate students' prior knowledge about shapes, she said, "Raise your hand if you know what this figure is called." She gave students some think time before calling on Dan.

"It's a quadrilateral because it has four sides," he said.

"You're right, Dan," Christine responded. "What else could we call this figure?"

"It's a square," Maria offered.

"Yes, you can also call it a *square,*" Christine said.

"This figure has lots of names: quadrilateral, square, polygon, and more, but today we're going to call it a *square.*"

Christine then held up a card with the word *square* written on it and placed it into a large pocket chart at the front of the room. To give the students a visual referent, she placed a square pattern block next to the word card in the pocket chart. Then she directed the students to say the word *square* together in a choral voice.

Next, Christine took a yellow hexagon from the bag of transparent pattern blocks and placed it onto the overhead. She asked the students if they knew the name of the figure.

"It's a hexagon," Julio said.

Christine placed a word card with *hexagon* written on it in the pocket chart. She had the students say the word aloud and then turned back to Julio. "Julio, tell us why it's a *hexagon.*"

"Because it has six sides and six vertices," he answered.

Touching each side of the hexagon with her index finger, Christine directed the students to each take a hexagon out of the zip-top bag on their desk and count the sides aloud with her to check if Julio was correct. She also had the students touch and count the vertices on the hexagon and on the square as well. Even though the students had learned the words *sides*, *vertex*, and *vertices* in a recent lesson on polygons, Christine reviewed the words with the students and placed the vocabulary words into the pocket chart for reference.

Christine continued to introduce each pattern block in the same way: she asked the students to name each block and touch and count the number of sides and vertices, then she placed a word card into the pocket chart with a pattern block next to it. When she was finished, the pocket chart looked like this:

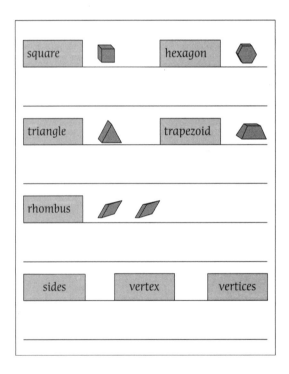

To review the pattern block shapes she'd introduced, Christine held up each block and had the students say the name aloud. When she got to the blue rhombus, Christine held up two of them.

"When there is one of these, we say *rhombus*," she said, emphasizing the vocabulary word. "But when there is more than one *rhombus*, we say *rhombi*."

Whenever possible, Christine takes the opportunity to develop students' English language skills during math class. In this case, she provided an example of another word and its plural form. "If you have one mouse, you say *mouse*," Christine continued. "But what if you have more than one mouse? What do we say?"

"Mice!" several students exclaimed.

Introducing Sentence Frames and Prepositions

Christine taped two sentence frames to the board that students had used in a previous lesson on polygons:

This is a _____. It is/has _____.

This is a _____ because _____.

Christine directed the students to practice reading the sentence frames aloud with her, pausing for the blank spaces. Then she modeled using one of the frames to describe the square pattern block. "This is a square. It has four sides," she said. "Raise your hand if you want to give us an example using another frame to describe one of the pattern blocks."

Cindy held up the yellow hexagon and said, "This is a hexagon because it has six sides."

"This is a square because it has four vertices," Julio volunteered.

"And four equal sides," Christine added. "You can add to your sentences to make the descriptions longer. For example, you could say, 'This square has four sides, four vertices, and four angles.'"

Next, Christine had partners practice using the sentence frames to describe the pattern blocks while she circulated around the room, listening in and supporting students when needed. Following is an exchange between Carolina, a beginning English speaker, and Ruth, an intermediate English speaker.

Carolina: This is a triangle because it has three sides equal.

Ruth: This is a hexagon because it has six angles.

Carolina: This is a square. It has four sides.

Ruth: This is a triangle. It has three equal sides.

The next exchange was between Diana, an intermediate English speaker, Cindy, an advanced English speaker, and Christine. Here,

Christine prompted Cindy to use correct academic language to describe the pattern block.

Diana: This is a hexagon. It has six sides.

Cindy: This is a quadrilateral because it has four sides, four vertices, and four corners.

Christine: Cindy, what do mathematicians call *corners*?

Cindy: This is a quadrilateral because it has four *angles*.

Christine: The quadrilateral you are holding is also called a . . .

Cindy: Trapezoid.

After the students had practiced describing the pattern blocks using the sentence frames, Christine asked for their attention and placed the word card *on* in the pocket chart.

"Pick up the green triangle and put it *on* your head," Christine directed as she modeled the action she wanted the students to do. As she said the word *on*, she pointed to the word in the pocket chart. Christine then directed the students to put the triangle *on* their desk.

Next, Christine placed the word *above* in the pocket chart and asked the students to put the triangle above their desk, above the floor, and above their partner's head. She introduced the words *below*, *to the right of*, and *to the left of* in the same manner.

When Christine was satisfied that students understood the meaning of the words, she told them that the words were called *prepositions*. Then she taped the following sentence frame to the board:

Put the _____ *on the* _____.
   above
   below
   to the right of
   to the left of	

Christine directed the students to practice saying the sentence frame aloud together, pausing for the blank spaces. She then said, "I might use the sentence frames to say, 'Put the square on the hexagon.'"

She asked the students to follow her direction. As they did, she quickly scanned the room to see if they were following.

"What if I switched it?" Christine asked. "Now put the hexagon on the square."

After the students followed her directions, she told them to put aside their pattern blocks and focus their attention on the screen at the front of the room. Christine placed one of each of the transparent pattern blocks on the overhead projector: a green triangle, a red trapezoid, a yellow hexagon, a blue rhombus, and a tan rhombus.

"I'm going to build a shape and describe how I build it using the sentence frames and the prepositions," she began. "For the *Build a Shape* game, I'm going to keep the blocks flat."

As Christine built her shape, she described what she was doing for the students: "Put the hexagon on the desk." (The overhead projector was serving as her desk.) "Put the square on the hexagon. Put the triangle to the right of the hexagon."

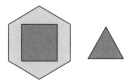

"What if I want the vertices of the triangle and the hexagon to touch?" Christine asked the class. "Talk to a partner about what I would have to do to the pattern blocks, and use the blocks at your desk to help you think."

When discussion died down, Christine called on Julio to come up to the overhead and show the class what to do. He rearranged the blocks so that they looked like this:

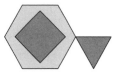

"So Julio rotated the hexagon and the triangle so that the vertices touch," Christine said, moving the blocks on the overhead to repeat what Julio had done. "And if I want the sides of the hexagon and the triangle to touch, I can rotate the triangle."

After Christine had modeled how to build a simple shape and described how she built it using the sentence frames and prepositions, she built another shape on the overhead with the light off, so the shape was hidden from the students' view.

Before she directed the class to build the shape on their desktops, Christine introduced two new sentence frames to provide a few more specific clues about her shape. She taped these sentence frames on the board and had the students read them aloud:

> The _____ should touch.

> The _____ of the _____ should touch the _____ of the _____.

The first frame is more basic, intended for beginning or intermediate English speakers. The second frame is more complicated and could be used by intermediate or advanced English speakers.

"I could use several sentence frames to give you directions for building my shape," Christine said. "I could say, 'Put the triangle on the desk. Put the square above the triangle. The sides should touch.' Or I could say, 'Put the triangle on the desk. Put the square above the triangle. The side of the triangle should touch the side of the square.'"

Christine repeated these directions while pointing to the words in the sentence frames and told the students to build the shape using their pattern blocks. Once they were finished, she turned on the overhead light to show the class her shape. The students cheered.

Christine built a few more examples on the overhead projector so that students could practice following her directions. She started with two blocks and then moved to three blocks, each time using the sentence frames to give directions. She also asked a student volunteer to build a shape on his desk and give directions using the sentence frames so that Christine could build the shape on the overhead. When she felt confident that the class had had enough practice, Christine told the students what they were going to do next.

Playing the Game

"Now you're going to work with a partner who is sitting next to you, and one person is going to build a shape using a file folder to hide the shape," she explained, holding up a folder and modeling how to place it between partners on a desk.

"One person will make a shape using two pattern blocks," she continued. "The pattern blocks have to be flat on your desk when you build, not standing up." Christine illustrated using a triangle.

"After you make the shape, use the sentence frames to help you explain to your partner how to build the shape. When your partner has finished building, look at his shape. If your partner's shape is not quite right, you need to explain how to fix it. When your partner's shape matches yours, remove the folder to show your shape. Then you're going to switch, and your partner will build a shape."

"Can we use more than two blocks for building?" Bernardo asked.

"Start with two blocks," Christine replied. "When you think you're ready, you can use more blocks to build with."

"Are we allowed to ask our partner questions while we're building their shape?" Amy asked.

"Sure," Christine responded. "The more you communicate or talk with your partner, the better!"

Christine was aware that her verbal directions might be difficult for some English learners to follow, so she asked a volunteer to rephrase what she'd said, providing students with another opportunity to comprehend the instructions. When it seemed that everyone understood what to do, Christine distributed one file folder to each pair of students and signaled everyone to begin.

Following is an exchange between Amy, an advanced English speaker, and Franco, a beginning English speaker. Amy built a shape first, hidden from Franco's view:

"Put the blue rhombus sideways," Amy directed. "Then put your square above the rhombus."

For her last direction, Amy used one of the sentence frames in the pocket chart to help her. She said, "The vertex of the rhombus should touch the side of the square."

Franco successfully created Amy's shape. Now it was Franco's turn to build. This is the shape he built on his desktop:

Before Franco began giving directions, he glanced at the pocket chart for assistance. "Put the hexagon on your desk. Put the square below the hexagon."

"Do the sides touch?" Amy asked.

Again, Franco used the sentence frames for support. "The sides should touch."

The two students seemed delighted at their success in giving and following directions. They were motivated to use the language of mathematics because there was a clear purpose in doing so.

Next, Amy built this shape using three pattern blocks:

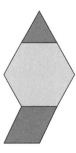

"First, put the hexagon on your desk," she directed. "Then put the triangle above it. Next, put your blue rhombus under the hexagon."

Amy strayed a bit from the sentence frames because she was ready to do so. In her directions, she used adverbs that order *first, then,* and *next*. The purpose of the sentence frames is to teach English learners new forms of language and to support them in using those forms, not to limit students who are ready to move beyond the frames.

When Amy had finished giving her directions, she checked the shape Franco had made:

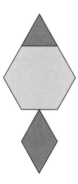

Amy realized that she needed to help Franco fix it, so she looked to the pocket chart for support. "Franco, the side of the rhombus should touch the side of the hexagon."

Franco fixed his design and then he built this new shape for Amy to make:

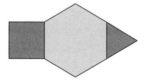

"Put the hexagon on the desk," Franco said. "Put the triangle on the side of the hexagon."

Amy interrupted Franco and asked, "On which side of the hexagon?"

Franco looked at the sentence frames, then he responded slowly but deliberately, "Put the triangle on the right side of the hexagon. Put the square on the left side of the hexagon. The sides should touch."

Amy smiled and finished building the exact same shape as Franco's.

Just as Amy was beginning to build another shape, time had run out, and Christine called the students back to attention.

Build a Shape, Part 1

"We've run out of time for today," Christine told the class. "Tomorrow we'll continue to build shapes with pattern blocks, but we'll be *writing* directions to our partner rather than *telling* our partner how to build our shapes." (See Chapter 4.)

Activity Directions ✦ **Build a Shape**

Minilesson Introducing Academic Language

1. Distribute a small plastic zip-top bag full of pattern blocks to each student. Allow students a few minutes to explore the blocks.

2. Introduce the square pattern block by placing a square block on the overhead projector. Have students take a square from their bag, say the name aloud together, and count the number of sides and vertices. Place a card with the word *square* on it into a pocket chart or tape it to the board. Place a square pattern block in the pocket chart next to the word card (or draw a picture of a square next to the word card taped to the board).

3. Place cards with the words *sides*, *vertex*, and *vertices* in the pocket chart or tape them to the board.

4. Introduce each of the remaining pattern blocks by repeating Step 2.

5. Introduce the first two sentence frames and have students say them aloud, pausing for the blank spaces:

> *This is a _____. It is/has _____.*

> *This is a _____ because _____.*

6. Have students practice using the sentence frames to describe the pattern blocks.

7. Using one of the pattern blocks, introduce the meaning of the prepositions (e.g., "Put the triangle *on* your head"; "Put the triangle *above* your desk"; "Put the triangle *to the right of* your desk"). Add the preposition word cards to the vocabulary chart.

8. Introduce the following sentence frame and have students read it aloud, pausing for the blank spaces:

> Put the _____ on the _____ .
>   above
>   below
>   to the right of
>   to the left of

9. Build a shape on the overhead projector using two pattern blocks. Describe the location of each shape using the prepositions and the sentence frame. Repeat this several times, using different blocks and different prepositions. Have the students build the shapes along with you.

10. Introduce the following sentence frames and have the students read them aloud:

> The _____ should touch.

> The _____ of the _____ should touch the _____ of the _____ .

11. Turn off the overhead projector light and build a shape using two or three pattern blocks. Use the sentence frames to describe for the class the location of the blocks. Direct the students to build the shape, then turn the overhead light on so they can check. Repeat this several times until students are comfortable with the location words.

Playing the Game

1. Distribute a file folder to each pair of students so that they can hide their shapes from one another. Explain how partners should play the game:

    a. One student builds a figure using only two pattern blocks and describes it to her partner using the sentence frames with the prepositions.

    b. The builder checks to see if her partner re-created the exact same shape. If not, the builder needs to describe how to fix it. When the shapes match, the builder reveals her shape.

    c. Partners switch roles.

    d. When they are ready, partners continue playing the game, building figures with three pattern blocks.

2. As students play the game, circulate to observe pairs and provide help as needed.

4 Build a Shape, Part 2

A Geometry Lesson

Overview

In *Build a Shape, Part 2*, students create a shape from pattern blocks and trace it onto a piece of paper. After tracing their shape, the students use prepositions and sequencing words to write directions for building their shape. Afterward, partners trade papers and try to build one another's shapes by following the written directions.

Math Goal: Students will be able to describe location and movement using common language and geometric language.

Language Goal: Students will be able to use prepositions to describe the location of specific pattern blocks. Students will use sequencing words to write directions for building a shape made from pattern blocks.

Key Vocabulary: above, after that, below, finally, first, hexagon, next, on, rhombus, sides, square, then, to the left of, to the right of, trapezoid, triangle, vertex, vertices

Materials

+ 1 set of overhead pattern blocks
+ 5 sentence strips or pieces of construction paper for sentence frames
+ 17 word cards for key vocabulary terms
+ pattern blocks, at least 1 of each block (hexagon, trapezoid, triangle, blue rhombus, tan rhombus) per student
+ small zip-top bags to hold pattern blocks, 1 per student
+ optional: pocket chart

Sentence Frames that Help Students Write Directions for Making Pattern Block Shapes

All Students

> *First,* _____ .

> *Next,* _____ .

> *Then,* _____ .

> *After that,* _____ .

> *Finally,* _____ .

Class Profile

Of the thirty students in Ms. Handel's class, half are native English speakers, and the other half of the class is made up of beginning, intermediate, and advanced English speakers.

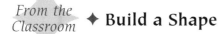

From the Classroom ✦ **Build a Shape**

Minilesson Introducing Academic Language

Christine began Part 2 of the *Build a Shape* lesson by creating a shape on the overhead projector and thinking aloud for the class as she placed each block, in sequential order, to make the shape. Each time she verbalized a direction for making her shape, Christine used the sentence frames and vocabulary that the students had learned in Part 1 of the lesson (see Chapter 3). In addition, Christine used the following sequencing words while describing the directions: *first*, *then*, and *finally*.

"I'm going to think out loud as I build my shape on the overhead," Christine told the class. She began building a shape with her transparent pattern blocks. "First, put the square on the table. Then, put the tan rhombus to the right of the square. The sides should be touching. Finally, put the blue rhombus to the left of the square. The sides should be touching." As she gave the directions, Christine spoke slowly, emphasizing the location words, the sequencing words, and the geometry vocabulary.

"Did you notice that I used the sentence frames we learned to describe how I made my shape?" Christine asked the class. "What other words did I use when I made the shape on the overhead?"

"You said what you did first, and next, and last," Julio noted.

"That's right," Christine acknowledged. "As a matter of fact, I used the words *first, then,* and *finally* to describe the order for the directions. These are sequencing words, words that tell the order of the directions."

Christine then put the following sentence frames in the pocket chart:

First, _____.

Next, _____.

Then, _____.

After that, _____.

Finally, _____.

Pointing to the sequencing words, she said, "These are the words I used and some other words that you can use when giving directions for making a shape with pattern blocks." She then directed the students to read aloud the new words she'd introduced.

To put the direction words in a familiar context, Christine said, "If we wanted to describe what we did yesterday in school, we could say, '*First* we read a book. *Then* we had circle time. *Next* we did an activity. *After that,* we went to PE, and *finally,* we went home.'"

Each time she used one of the sequencing words, Christine pointed to the word in the pocket chart, saying it with emphasis. Using words in familiar contexts is one way to make content comprehensible to English learners.

To further illustrate the meaning of the sequencing words, Christine pointed to one student at a time and said, "First, Franco may go to lunch.

Next, Julio may go. Then, Cynthia may go. After that, Carlos may go to lunch. And finally, Ms. Handel may go."

After giving students a few examples for using the new sequencing words, Christine had the students practice using the words with a partner.

When students were finished, Christine cleared the overhead projector of pattern blocks. She then told the students that they were going to help her give directions for making a new shape, using the sentence frames containing location words they'd learned in Part 1 of the *Build a Shape* lesson and the new sequencing words in the pocket chart.

Christine began by placing a triangle on the overhead and saying, "First . . . ," and then pausing for the students to use the sentence frames to help her complete the direction.

"Put the triangle on the table," the students chorused.

Christine then placed the square below the triangle and said, "Next . . . ,"

"Put the square below the triangle," several students said.

"And the sides should touch!" Cynthia added with expression.

After placing the hexagon on the overhead, Christine said, "Finally . . . ,"

Several students completed Christine's direction, saying, "Put the hexagon below the square and the sides should touch!"

When she was finished, Christine wrote the directions on the board for making her shape and directed the students to read the sentences aloud:

1. *First, put the triangle on the table.*
2. *Next, put the square below the triangle. The sides should touch.*
3. *Finally, put the hexagon below the square. The sides should touch.*

The Lesson: Writing and Following Directions for Building Shapes

After modeling how to write directions for making a pattern block shape, Christine made sure she had everyone's attention before explaining what students were to do next. "I'm going to pass out the pattern blocks," she began. "I want each of you to build a shape using the blocks. Choose the number of blocks that you feel comfortable using."

Christine held up a piece of white paper and continued, "Make your shape on this paper and trace the blocks. Then, turn your paper over and write directions for making your shape. When writing your directions, use the sentence frames to help you."

"Do we have to use all the words?" Diana asked.

"Use the sentence frames that make sense to you," Christine replied. "You can use some of the sequencing words or all of them if you want. Remember to write your directions carefully. When you're finished, you're going to trade with a partner and see if you can build each other's shapes by following the written directions."

The students were excited and got right to work, making shapes with their pattern blocks, then tracing the shapes, and finally writing directions for building their shapes.

As Christine circulated, she noticed that in general, students who were beginning or intermediate speakers of English, like Allen, used fewer pattern blocks, simpler sentence frames, and fewer sequencing words. (See Figure 4–1.) Having the sentence frames available provided the students with the support they needed in order to produce language in English.

Tierra, another intermediate speaker, used descriptors that made following the directions easy. As Tierra worked, she looked up at the sequencing words in the pocket chart and the sentence frames on the board for guidance. Once she finished writing, she read her directions back to Christine, checking to see if they were correct. (See Figure 4–2.)

Dorothea, an intermediate-level English speaker, used four pattern blocks and all but one of the sequencing words in her written directions. (See Figure 4–3.)

Amy, an advanced English speaker, used all six pattern blocks and all of the sequencing words in her written directions. (See Figure 4–4.)

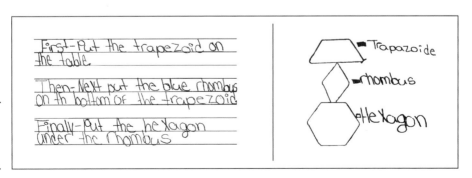

FIGURE 4-1. Allen used a few pattern blocks and simple sentence frames.

First- Put the trapezoid on the table.

Then- Next put the blue rhombus on th bottom of the trapezoid

Finally- Put the hexagon under the rhombus

First, Put the hexagon on the
table but the hexagon have to be flat.

Then, Put the trapezoid
below the hexagon the Short way
and touching Side.

Findily, Put the triangle above The
hexagon touching Side.

FIGURE 4-2.
Tierra used
descriptors to
help with her
directions.

FirSt, put your Hecagon on the tabole
then above the hecagon put your triangel the
Botom Shoud touch   Next put
the square totheRight of the Hecagon finaly
put the trapazoid Balow theHeagon the
Short part Shoud touch.

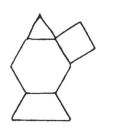

FIGURE 4-3.
Dorothea
used several
pattern
blocks and
quite a few
sequencing
words in her
directions.

First, put the Hexagon on table
then, put blue rombus above the hexagon the sides touch.
Next, put the Square above the bleu rombus sides touch.
After that, put the triangle left of square sides touch.
now, put the trapezoid on the right of the hexagon
and the blue rombus the Short Side Shoud touch
blue rombus.
Finally, put the white rombus on top of trapezoid
Sides Shoud touch.

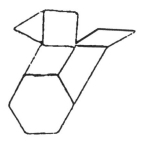

FIGURE 4-4.
Amy used all
six pattern
blocks and
all of the
sequencing
words in her
directions.

FIGURE 4-5.
Florence
found that
using sen-
tence frames
helped
enhance her
directions.

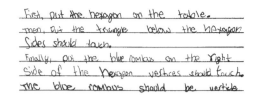

First, put the hexagon on the table.
Then, put the triangle below the hexagon.
Sides should touch.
Finally, put the blue rhombus on the right
side of the hexagon, vertices should touch.
The blue rhombus should be vertical.

Providing several sentence frames of different levels of difficulty serves to meet the needs of students with varying levels of English language proficiency.

The sentence frames are also useful for native English speakers, like Florence. She used the frames to help her write directions, adding an additional piece of helpful information at the end: *The blue rhombus should be vertical.* (See Figure 4–5.)

As students finished their tracings and the written directions, they began to trade their work with other students who were finished. There was much excitement in the room as students read directions and tried to build their partner's shape. When students needed help reading or deciphering what was written, partners readily assisted each other. While the students worked, Christine circulated throughout the room, giving assistance when necessary.

Twin Goals: English Language Development and Math Understanding

Build a Shape involved Ms. Handel's students in giving and following directions verbally and in writing. Students were able to develop and use their knowledge of geometric shapes, and they learned to describe location and movement using the language of geometry. At the same time, the students were learning to use location and sequencing words in a meaningful context. *Build a Shape* is an example of how mathematical knowledge is developed through language and how language abilities can be developed through mathematics instruction.

*Activity
Directions* ◆ **Build a Shape**

1. Build a shape on the overhead projector using pattern blocks. Describe for the students the position of each shape using the prepositions and sentence frames introduced in the first *Build a Shape* lesson.

As you build the shape, also describe for the students the order in which you place the blocks. For example:

> *First*, put the hexagon on the table.
>
> *Next*, put the triangle to the right of the hexagon. The sides should touch.
>
> *Then*, put the square to the left of the hexagon. The sides should touch.
>
> *After that*, put the blue rhombus below the hexagon. The sides should touch.
>
> *Finally*, put the tan rhombus above the hexagon. The sides should touch.

2. Place the sequencing sentence frames in a pocket chart or tape them to the board. Use the words in a few examples with familiar contexts to help students understand them.

3. Build a second shape on the overhead projector with the pattern blocks. As you place each block on the overhead, elicit from students sentences to describe the location of the block using the prepositions. Record their ideas on the overhead or chart paper. For example, say, "First . . . ," and have students complete the sentence; say, "Next . . ." and have students complete the sentence; and so on until you have completed the shape. Then have the class read the written directions aloud together.

4. Distribute pattern blocks to students, ensuring that they have at least one of each block.

5. Using pattern blocks, students each build a figure using a certain number of blocks and trace the shape on their paper. On the other side of the paper, have them record each step of their directions using the sentence frames to guide their writing.

6. Have students trade papers and try to duplicate each other's figures by reading the directions.

5 Roll Two Dice

A Probability Lesson

Overview

Prior to this probability lesson, students are introduced to vocabulary words that they will need to describe data and make predictions and draw conclusions about data.

Then students play a game, *Roll Two Dice*, in which they think about the probability of the sums generated when rolling two dice. After listing the possible sums that can be rolled with two dice (2 to 12), the students work individually to roll the dice and record the combinations they roll on a chart, continuing until one sum reaches the finish line. Students describe what happened in their games and are taught various sentence frames to help them draw conclusions and then make new predictions.

Math Goal: Students will describe events as likely or unlikely; make predictions about the probability of the outcomes of simple experiments; and propose and justify conclusions that are based on data.

Language Goal: Students will make predictions and draw conclusions based on data.

Key Vocabulary: combination, combinations, dice, die, least, likely, most, predict, prediction, sum, sums, unlikely, way, ways

Materials

+ pairs of different-colored dice, 1 pair per student
+ 1 sheet of chart paper for key vocabulary terms
+ large two-column chart with the headings Likely and Unlikely
+ several sentence strips containing a variety of likely and unlikely statements

- ✦ 1 overhead transparency of the *Roll Two Dice* record sheet (see Blackline Masters)
- ✦ 9 sentence strips or pieces of construction paper for sentence frames
- ✦ *Roll Two Dice* record sheets, 1 per student

Sentence Frames That Help Students Make Predictions

Beginning

> *I predict that* _____ *will win.*

Intermediate/Advanced

> *I predict that* _____ *will win because* _____ .

Sentence Frames That Support Drawing Conclusions and Making New Predictions

Beginning

> *If we play* Roll Two Dice *again,* _____ *is/are likely to win.*

> *If we play* Roll Two Dice *again,* _____ *is/are unlikely to win.*

Intermediate/Advanced

> *If we play* Roll Two Dice *again,* _____ *is/are likely to win because* _____ .

> *If we play* Roll Two Dice *again,* _____ *is/are unlikely to win because* _____ .

Class Profile

Of the thirty-three students in Mrs. Shore's class, eighteen are English language learners (ELLs), nine are native English speakers, and six have recently been reclassified by the school's English language program from English language learners to fluent English proficient. Most of the ELLs in the class are at the intermediate or advanced level of

English language proficiency. There are, however, a few students who are at the beginning level.

✦ **Roll Two Dice, Day 1**

Minilesson Introducing Academic Language

Christine Sphar greeted the students in Mrs. Shore's class and told them that she would be introducing a game that involved probability, an area of math. Smiles lit up across the room. Christine is a frequent visitor to room 15, where she helps students develop their English language skills. She usually teaches language arts, but today she would be teaching math.

"Today I'm going to teach you a game that uses dice," Christine began as she held up a pair of different-colored dice for the students to see. She then said, "Raise your hand if you've ever used dice."

After all the students acknowledged that they had experience with dice, Christine held up the dice again and explained, "When we have two or more, we say *dice*, but when we have only one, we say *die*. Sounds funny, doesn't it?"

Christine held up two dice, then one die, and directed the students to say the words aloud in a choral voice. She then wrote the words on a vocabulary chart that was affixed to the chalkboard.

Next, Christine wrote the word *sum* on the vocabulary chart and told the students that during the math game today, they would have to find the sums they could make when rolling two dice.

"Raise your hand if you can tell us what the word *sum* means," Christine directed, emphasizing the word while pointing to it on the vocabulary chart.

"It's the answer to an addition problem," Dan explained.

"That's right," Christine verified. She then wrote this equation on the chalkboard:

$$4 + 3 = 7$$

"Think about which number in this equation is the *sum*," she said to the class.

After a few seconds, she told the students to say the sum together in a choral voice as she pointed to the 7 in the equation.

"Raise your hand if you can spell the other word that sounds exactly like *sum,* but has a different meaning and a different spelling," Christine said.

After giving the students some think time, Christine called on Rafi, who spelled the word *some* aloud for the class as Christine wrote it on the board.

To illustrate the different meanings of the two words, Christine used them in sentences:

- ✦ I have *some* dice in my hand.
- ✦ This is the *sum* of four plus three.

Some of the words that we use to describe mathematical ideas have nonmathematical homonyms (words that sound the same and have the same spelling but have different meanings, like *odd*) and homophones (words that sound the same but are spelled differently and have different meanings, like *sum* and *some*). Pointing out these features of language in math class helps clarify the meanings of words for English language learners.

Christine again pointed to the equation she had written on the board:

$$4 + 3 = 7$$

"Four plus three is a *way* to make seven," she said, putting emphasis on the new vocabulary word. "Four plus three is a *combination* that makes the sum of seven."

After writing the words *way* and *combination* on the vocabulary chart, Christine asked the class, "What's another *way* to make seven? What's another *combination* that will make seven?"

"Six plus one makes seven," Brianna offered.

On the board, Christine wrote:

$$6 + 1$$

"So six plus one is another *way* to make seven," Christine said, emphasizing the new word. "Six plus one is another *combination* that makes seven. So now we have two *ways,* or *combinations,* that make the *sum* of seven." Christine added the words *ways* and *combinations* to the vocabulary chart.

Next, Christine taped a chart to the chalkboard that looked like this:

Likely	Unlikely

"I'm going to show you some sentences, and you're going to tell me what's *likely* to happen and what's *unlikely* to happen," Christine told the class. She added the terms to the vocabulary chart and then held up a sentence strip that read:

> *We will eat lunch today.*

Christine directed the students to read the sentence first silently to themselves and then aloud in a choral voice.

After the students read the sentence aloud, Christine said, "It is *likely* that we will eat lunch today. *Likely* means it will probably happen, or there's a good chance that it will happen."

Christine then taped the sentence strip onto the chart under the Likely column and directed the class to say the following sentence aloud in a choral voice: "It is likely that we will eat lunch today."

"Why is it likely that we will eat lunch today?" Christine asked.

"'Cause every day we eat lunch," Niki responded.

"Could something happen that might keep us from eating lunch today?" Christine probed.

"If there was a hurricane maybe we would have to go home!" Siera exclaimed. Everyone laughed.

"Yep, we probably would have to go home," said Christine, smiling. "So it's possible that we might not have lunch, but it's *likely* that we will, right?"

The students nodded in agreement.

Christine held up another sentence strip that read:

> *It will snow in San Diego this week.*

After having the students read the sentence silently and then aloud, Christine asked them if it was likely or unlikely to snow in San Diego this week.

The students all responded, "Unlikely!"

"It could snow if it got really, really, really cold," Christine clarified. "It's winter, and even in Southern California, it snows in some places. But this week, it's unlikely that it will snow."

After Christine taped the sentence strip under the Unlikely column on the chart, she continued to introduce sentences to students, first having them consider whether the event was likely to happen or unlikely to happen, and then asking students to explain why an event was likely or unlikely before taping the sentence strip under the correct column. Using the vocabulary words *likely* and *unlikely* in familiar contexts helped make the words accessible to English language learners.

When she was finished, the chart looked like this:

Likely	Unlikely
We will eat lunch today. We will play outside today. The principal will come into our room today. We will read books today. We will go home after school today.	It will snow this week in San Diego. An astronaut will come into our room today in his space suit. We will learn to fly an airplane today. Someone in our class will win a million dollars tomorrow.

Introducing the Game

To introduce the probability game *Roll Two Dice*, Christine wrote the name of the game on the chalkboard and directed the students to say the name aloud. To physically model the question she was posing, Christine held up a pair of dice in her hand, rolled them on Mrs. Shore's desk, and asked, "If I take these two dice and roll them on the tabletop, what sums could I roll?"

Christine had the students think for a few seconds and then called on Roberto.

"You could end up with seven when you roll the two dice," he said.

"Yes," Christine acknowledged. "Before, we said that one way to make seven is four plus three, and another way is six plus one. Those are two different ways, or combinations, that make seven. What other sums could we make when rolling two dice?"

"You could get nine," Dalia offered.

"How could you get nine?" Christine probed. "What *combination* makes nine?" Christine deliberately used the vocabulary word that was introduced in the minilesson, pointing to the word on the chart.

"Six plus three is one way," Dalia responded.

"And five plus four," Jessica added.

"When I roll two dice, could I get a *sum* of thirteen?" Christine asked the class. "I'll give you five seconds of think time."

When the time was up, Christine called on Lili, whose English language skills are at an intermediate level.

"You can't get a thirteen because there aren't enough numbers," she said.

Pushing Lili to use math vocabulary and to be more specific in her explanation, Christine asked, "What do we call the thirteen?"

"You can't get a *sum* of thirteen," Lili replied.

Christine then prompted, "There aren't enough numbers on the . . ."

"There aren't enough numbers on the dice to get a sum of thirteen," Lili said, completing Christine's prompt.

"What's the greatest number on each die?" Christine asked.

"Six!" the students chorused.

Christine continued, "So to get a thirteen, we'd need a number greater than six on the die, right?"

"Like seven plus six," Jazmin noted.

"Or eight plus five," added Brad.

Christine then posed the question again, "What sums are possible when you roll two dice?" She gave students a few minutes to discuss the question with a neighbor and then called the class back to attention.

"Thumbs up if you agree, thumbs down if you disagree, and thumbs sideways if you're not sure," Christine said to the class, modeling her directions using her thumb.

She began, "You can get a sum of thirteen when you roll two dice." All thumbs were turned down.

"You can get a sum of fourteen," she continued. Again, all thumbs were down.

"How about fifteen?" she asked. Once again, there was consensus in the class that this sum wasn't possible.

"What other sums are possible when rolling two dice?" Christine asked.

"You can get a sum of two," Jaz said.

"How? What way can you get a sum of two?" Christine probed.

"'Cause the smallest number on each die is one, and one plus one is two," Jaz explained. "You can't get a sum of one because there's no zero on the dice."

"What other sums are possible?" Christine asked.

The students generated a list of sums from 2 to 12. As they reported their ideas, Christine recorded the sums on the board like this:

2   3   4   5   6   7   8   9   10   11   12

To explain how to play the game, Christine placed an overhead transparency of the *Roll Two Dice* record sheet on the overhead projector. She pointed to the numbers 2 through 12 along the top of the record sheet and asked the students if they recognized the numbers. "What do you think these numbers stand for?" Christine asked.

"Those are the sums that you can get when you roll the two dice," Rob said.

"Yes," Christine replied. "Those are the sums. For this game, each person will get his own record sheet and two dice. To play the game, you should follow these directions."

Christine wrote the following directions on the board and then read them aloud:

1. *Roll the dice.*
2. *Add the numbers that come up.*
3. *Write down the combination, or way to make the sum, in the box below the sum.*
4. *Roll until one sum gets to the finish line.*

Christine rolled a red die and a green die a few times to show students how to record the combinations to make different sums. When modeling, she explained that it was important to write the number that came up on the red die first and the number on the green die second. This way, students would be able to see that 2 + 4 and 4 + 2, for example, are two different events. (See Figure 5–1.)

Making Predictions and Introducing Sentence Frames

Next, Christine asked the students to predict which sum they thought would win the race.

Roll Two Dice

2	3	4	5	6	7	8	9	10	11	12
	1 + 2	2 + 2		4 + 2			5 + 4			6 + 6
				2 + 4						
Finish Line										

FIGURE 5-1.
Sample *Roll Two Dice* record sheet

"Raise your hand if you know what a prediction is," she asked as she wrote the words *predict* and *prediction* on the vocabulary chart. She had the students say the words aloud several times as she pointed to them.

"It's like a guess," Mohammed answered.

"You're right, Mohammed, a prediction is like a guess," she acknowledged. "We also make predictions when we read; we predict what's going to happen in a story. In science, we predict what will happen in an experiment. For *Roll Two Dice*, I want you to predict or guess which sum will win the race."

Christine taped the following sentence frame, intended for beginning ELLs, to the board and had the students read it aloud, pausing for the blank space:

> *I predict that _____ will win.*

Several volunteers offered to make predictions using the sentence frame.

Alberto, a beginning English speaker, shared, "I predict that three will win."

Augustin said, "I predict that four will win."

After a few other students offered their predictions, Christine had everyone turn to a partner and share their predictions, using the sentence frame on the board. When the students had finished, Christine handed out a red die, a green die, and a record sheet to each student, and play began.

As the students played the game, Christine circulated, observing students. As she passed by Dan, she overheard his surprise at rolling snake eyes.

"Wow! Snake eyes!" he exclaimed. Dan is a native English speaker and is very articulate when explaining his math thinking.

"Why are you surprised?" Christine asked.

"Because it doesn't happen very often. It's unlikely to roll double ones because you can only get it one way," he responded. Dan's remark is an example of how language can be used to convey mathematical understanding. It's the kind of talk that Christine looks for and expects from all of her students, including those students for whom English is a second language.

After five minutes or so, most students were about halfway finished with the game. Christine signaled for them to stop playing and told them that they now had an opportunity to change their predictions based on the information they had gathered from their game so far. She then taped the following sentence frame, intended for intermediate and advanced ELLs, to the board:

I predict that _____ will win because _____.

"Who can remind us what a *prediction* is?" Christine asked.

"It's like a guess," Cris said.

Christine then directed the students to read this new frame aloud in a choral voice, pausing for the blank spaces. She asked the students to look at their record sheets and think about their predictions.

After several seconds, Christine asked for a few volunteers to share their predictions with the class. Brad went first. "I predict that seven will win," he said, using the beginning-level frame.

"I predict that eight will win," Autumn said.

"I predict that seven will win because it's closer to the finish line," Gaby said, using the frame that prompted an explanation.

"I predict that six will win because I keep rolling it," Mary shared.

"Now turn to your neighbor and share your new predictions," Christine told the students. "Use the sentence frame that you're most comfortable with."

Partner talk at this point gave everyone a chance to practice using language to make predictions. As Christine circulated, she noticed that for the most part, students were using sentence frames that were appropriate for their language level. Most of the native English speakers and more advanced English language learners were using the frames that prompted some explanation. There were some advanced English speakers who relied on the more basic frame. In these cases, Christine pushed for an explanation if appropriate.

When Christine noticed that beginning English speakers needed support and encouragement to produce language, she provided it. Following is an interaction between Christine and Mohammed, an intermediate English speaker, and Alberto, a beginning English speaker. Christine used prompts, questions, and rephrasing to help the two students discuss their predictions.

Christine: Which sum do you think is likely to win?

Mohammed: I think seven.

Christine: Why do you think seven will win?

Mohammed: 'Cause it's close.

Christine: Seven is close to . . .

Mohammed: Seven is close to the finish line.

Christine: Which sum do you think will win, Alberto?

Alberto: I predict that seven will win [*using the sentence frame for support*].

Christine: Why? Why do you think it's likely that seven will win?

Alberto: It has lots of numbers. It's almost finish.

Christine: So you think seven is likely to win because it has lots of ways to make it and it's almost at the finish line?

Alberto: Yes, it's almost at the finish line.

When the talk died down, Christine addressed the class. "Alberto said that he thought that seven will win because it's closer to the finish line. Why do you think some sums are getting closer to the finish line than others?" Christine asked this question to push for more explanations from students. After waiting a few seconds, she called on Niki.

"Because it comes up more. Seven is coming up more on my game and that's why it's closer to the finish line," she explained.

"But why?" Christine probed.

"Because seven is a lucky number," Manuel said.

"Other ideas?" Christine asked.

"Seven is going to win because it has more *factors*," Jaz reasoned.

Mrs. Shore's class had just begun a unit on factors and multiples the previous week. It isn't uncommon for students to misuse or misapply new vocabulary they are learning. Recognizing this, Christine responded with a question to clarify. "Jaz, when we roll two dice, do we add or multiply the numbers that come up?"

"Add," he responded.

"So the numbers on the dice aren't *factors*; they are called *addends*," Christine explained with a light touch. "If we were multiplying, you would be correct. Can you think of another way to say what you said instead of using the word *factors*?"

"I predict seven will win because it has more numbers that add up to seven," he said.

"That makes sense to me," Christine responded in a reassuring tone.

Describing the Results

After students revised their predictions, Christine directed them to complete their games. When they were finished playing, she asked for their attention.

"When I call out one of the *sums*, I want you to stand up if that *sum* won your race." She added *sums* to the vocabulary chart and then began calling out numbers.

As students stood up, Christine had two volunteers count winning sums while she tallied them on the board like this:

```
                       IIII III   JHT

        II             III  JHT JHT  II    I     I

  2     3     4    5    6     7     8    9    10    11    12
```

The students seemed surprised that some sums, like 2, 3, 5, 11, and 12, never won a race. When the sum of 7 was called out, more than half the class stood up. This caused a stir.

"What do you notice?" Christine asked.

"Seven won a lot!" Augustin observed.

"Two and twelve didn't win ever!" Siera exclaimed.

On the vocabulary chart, Christine wrote the words *most* and *least*. Now the vocabulary chart looked like this:

predict   sum
prediction   sums
dice   way
die   ways
likely   combination
unlikely   combinations
                 most
                 least

Next, Christine held up Gaby's record sheet for everyone to see. (See Figure 5–2.) "On Gaby's sheet, the sums that were rolled the *most* were six, seven, and eight," she said, pointing first to the columns on Gaby's sheet and then to the word *most* on the vocabulary chart.

Still holding up Gaby's sheet, Christine continued, "See how the sums of eleven, twelve, two, three, and four were rolled the *least*." Using Gaby's record sheet as an example gave the students a visual clue for the meaning of the words *least* and *most*.

"What happened the *most* and the *least* on your record sheets?" Christine asked.

Roll Two Dice

2	3	4	5	6	7	8	9	10	11	12
1+1	2+1		3+2	4+2	6+1	6+2	6+3	6+4	5+6	6+6
1+1	2+1		2+3	4+2	5+7	5+3	6+3	6+4		
	2+1		3+2	3+3	4+3	4+4	5+4	5+5		
	2+1		3+2	3+3	5+2	6+2	6+3	5+5		
			4+1	3+3	5+2	5+3	6+3	5+5		
			4+1	4+2	5+2	6+2	4+5	6+4		
			4+1	5+1	4+3	5+3	6+3	6+4		
			3+2	3+3	4+3	4+4	6+3	5+5		
			4+1	4+2	4+3	5+3	5+4	5+5		
				4+6	6+1	6+2				
				3+3	6+1	5+3				
					5+2					

Finish Line

FIGURE 5–2. Gaby's record sheet.

"Seven and eight came up the most," Kim reported.

"Two, twelve, three, and four came up the least," Lili added.

"Ten came up the most on mine!" Siera exclaimed.

After a few more volunteers had reported, Christine directed students to share with a neighbor about the sums that came up the *most* and *least* in their games. She urged them to use the vocabulary words *most* and *least* in their descriptions.

When students were finished sharing, Christine collected their record sheets and told the students they'd continue with the lesson tomorrow.

✦ Roll Two Dice, Day 2

Christine distributed students' record sheets and wrote the possible sums on the chalkboard:

2   3   4   5   6   7   8   9   10   11   12

"Yesterday, we found that there are different ways to make each of the sums," Christine began. "Let's start with the sum of two. Yesterday, we noticed that the sum of two wasn't rolled very often."

"That's because you can't roll a two," Roberto said.

"You can't?" Christine asked.

"I mean, it's unlikely," Roberto said, revising his thought.

"How can you make a sum of two when you roll two dice?" Christine asked the class.

"One plus one," Alberto offered.

Christine was pleased to see Alberto contributing to the conversation. He is a beginning English speaker and has been in the United States for only one year. While playing *Roll Two Dice*, Alberto was fully engaged and seemed eager to talk about the game with his neighbors. Games can be an effective way to motivate English learners. Games also provide an informal and nonthreatening context for talking about mathematical ideas.

"Any other way to make the sum of two, Alberto?" Christine asked.

"No, only one plus one," he replied.

Christine recorded the number combination below the sum of 2 on the chalkboard:

2   3   4   5   6   7   8   9   10   11   12

1 + 1

Roll Two Dice

"What about the sum of three?" Christine asked.

"You can do two plus one," Tina began. "But you can also do one plus two."

If Tina hadn't brought up the idea that 2 + 1 and 1 + 2 are two different events, Christine would have done so. Understanding that 1 + 2 and 2 + 1 are different events when rolling two dice can be difficult for students. Using two different colors of dice when playing the game can help students understand this idea.

Christine continued with another example, "So according to Tina's theory, you can make the *sum* of four by rolling a three and a one and one and a three?"

Students nodded in agreement.

To check for further understanding, Christine asked, "Can I make a sum of four by rolling a four and a zero?"

"No!" Dan exclaimed. "There's no zero on the dice."

Christine continued to call on different students to provide her with all the different ways to make the sums 2 through 12. When she was finished, the chart looked like this:

2	3	4	5	6	7	8	9	10	11	12
1+1	1+2	2+2	3+2	3+3	5+2	4+4	5+4	5+5	5+6	6+6
	2+1	1+3	2+3	2+4	2+5	5+3	4+5	6+4	6+5	
		3+1	4+1	4+2	3+4	3+5	3+6	4+6		
			1+4	5+1	4+3	2+6	6+3			
				1+5	6+1	6+2				
					1+6					

"Look at the chart and talk with your neighbor about what you notice," Christine directed.

After about a minute, Christine called the students back to attention and asked for their ideas.

"It's a pattern," Roberto said. "It goes from least to most."

Christine was pleased that Roberto was using the vocabulary taught in the lesson to describe the data.

"It looks like a city full of buildings if you look at it upside down!" Cassie observed.

"Seven has the most," Rob noted.

Drawing Conclusions and Making New Predictions

Next, Christine told the students that she wanted them to think about the game of *Roll Two Dice* and draw some conclusions and make new predictions. "When we draw conclusions in science, we look at what happened in an experiment and come up with ideas about it," Christine explained. "I want you to think about what you've learned from playing *Roll Two Dice*, then make a new prediction."

Christine wrote the following questions on the board and had the students read them aloud:

✦ *If we play* Roll Two Dice *again, which sum or sums are likely to win?*
✦ *Which sum or sums are unlikely to win?*

Christine then taped the following sentence frames to the board and had the students read them aloud, pausing for the blank spaces:

> *If we play* Roll Two Dice *again,* _____ *is/are likely to win.*

> *If we play* Roll Two Dice *again,* _____ *is/are unlikely to win.*

> *If we play* Roll Two Dice *again,* _____ *is/are likely to win because* _____ .

> *If we play* Roll Two Dice *again,* _____ *is/are unlikely to win because* _____ .

After partners practiced using the sentence frames to share their conclusions and new predictions, Christine told the students that she wanted them to write about their thinking on the back of their *Roll Two Dice* record sheets. She encouraged the students to use the sentence frames to help them with their writing.

As Christine circulated, she listened in on conversations and asked several students to read to her what they had written. She encouraged the students to share their writing with their neighbors when they were finished.

Jessica and Alberto are both beginning English speakers. Christine was impressed with Jessica because she used one of the sentence frames that prompted an explanation of her thinking. Although her explanation needed some editing for syntax errors, she conveyed what she meant and understood. (See Figure 5–3.)

Alberto also chose one of the sentence frames that prompted an explanation. Like Jessica, his writing had syntax problems (and spelling errors), but they didn't get in the way of his conveying mathematical understanding. Christine recognizes that one of her roles is to model and give students feedback about grammar and syntax so that they develop their English language skills. At the same time, she doesn't want students' linguistic mistakes to inhibit the recognition of good mathematical thinking. (See Figure 5–4.)

Lili is an intermediate English language learner. Although she strayed just a bit from the sentence frames, her writing was

Roll Two Dice

2	3	4	5	6	7	8	9	10	11	12
1+1	2+1	3+1	4+1	5+1	5+2	5+3	6+3	6+4	5+6	
		2+2	3+2	5+1	6+1	4+4	6+3	6+4	6+5	
		2+2	4+1	4+2	6+1	6+2	5+4	5+5		
		2+2	4+1	4+2	4+3	6+2	5+4	4+6		
		3+1	3+2	4+2	5+2	6+2	5+4	6+4		
		3+1	4+1	4+2	4+3	6+2	5+4	5+5		
		3+1	3+2		5+2	6+2		6+4		
		3+1	3+2			5+3		5+5		
		3+1								
		3+1								
		2+2								
		3+1								

Finish Line

I think that four is unlikely to win because
It doesn't has a lot of number to sum with it.

FIGURE 5-3. Jessica, a beginning English speaker, stretched herself with this writing.

If I play Roll two Dice I thing seven is likely two win because it has to much ways to get seven. And two is unlikely two win because it has yust one way to win.

FIGURE 5-4. Alberto explained his thinking.

grammatically correct and showed mathematical understanding. Her work is notable because the way she has expressed herself sounds very much like a fluent English speaker. (See Figure 5–5.)

Jaz is a native English speaker. He used key vocabulary and the structure of the sentence frame in his explanation. (See Figure 5–6.)

Chris, another native English speaker, revealed some interesting thinking in his writing. His observation shows that he was beginning to think about assigning probabilities to the events using fractions. (See Figure 5–7.)

Siera, another native English speaker, was the only student in the class that had the sum of 10 as a winner. She's an example of a native English speaker who used part of a sentence frame to guide her, but for the most part wrote freely about her thinking. She was convinced that 10 would win the next time she played the game, even though she realized that there aren't a lot of ways to roll that sum! (See Figure 5–8.)

When the students were finished sharing their stories with one another, Christine asked for volunteers to read aloud their writing for the class to hear. This whole-class sharing brought closure to the lesson.

> I think that the sums that will win next time we Play Roll Two Dice are 7 and 8 because they have more ways to add the numbers. I think that the Sums that are unlikely to to win next time we Play Roll Two Dice are the Sums 2 and 12 because they have only one way to add.

FIGURE 5-5. Lili, an intermediate ELL, expressed herself like a fluent English speaker.

> If we play roll two dice again, seven is likely to win due to the fact that it has more ways or combinations than the other numbers. Then the numbers 2, 11, and 12 are unlikely to win because they have less ways or combinations.

FIGURE 5-6. Jaz, a native English speaker, used more sophisticated language to describe his thinking.

Roll Two Dice

Roll Two Dice

2	3	4	5	6	7	8	9	10	11	12
	2+1	3+1	3+2	4+2	6+1	6+2	6+3	6+4	6+5	6+6
		3+1	4+1	4+2	6+1	5+3	5+4	6+4	6+5	
		3+1	4+1	4+2	5+2	5+3		6+4	6+5	
		2+2	4+1	5+1	4+3	6+2		5+5	6+5	
			4+1	5+1	6+1	6+2		6+4		
			4+1	4+2	4+3	6+2		6+4		
			3+2	4+2	4+3	4+4		6+4		
			4+1	3+3	4+3	4+4		5+5		
						6+2				
						6+5				
						4+3				
						4+3				

Finish Line

I think that 8 is most likely to coin because 8 occured 12 times out of 56 rolls.

FIGURE 5-7. Chris's writing revealed some beginning ideas about probability.

I think 10n is likely to win because, it is 10 s turn to win because one persom won it that is me, but 7 alread won. If we play Roll the dice again all the rest of the numbers are not going to win but I know ten is going to win because 10 doesn't have alot of numbers to add t it, but, I know it is going to win. I can feel it. That is only if we play agian.

FIGURE 5-8. Siera was sure that the sum of 10 would win next time.

Activity Directions ✦ **Roll Two Dice**

Day 1

Minilesson Introducing Academic Language

1. Introduce the words *die* and *dice* to students. Record the words on a vocabulary chart and continue doing so for each new vocabulary word introduced.

2. Ask students to explain the word *sum*. Write an equation on the board (e.g., *4 + 3 = 7*) and ask students to identify the sum, or answer, in the equation.

3. Point to the equation $4 + 3 = 7$ and tell students that $4 + 3$ is one *way*, or *combination*, to make the sum of 7. Talk about other combinations that make 7.

4. Show the students a two-column chart labeled like this:

Likely	Unlikely

Show the students a sentence strip containing a statement that is likely to be true. For example:

> *We will eat lunch today.*

Read the sentence aloud with the class. Tell the students, "It is likely that we will eat lunch today." Have them repeat the sentence and then tape the strip under the Likely column in the chart.

5. Show students an unlikely statement, such as this:

> *It will snow this week.*

Read the sentence aloud with the class. Tell the students, "It is unlikely that it will snow this week." Have them repeat the sentence and then tape the strip in the Unlikely column on the chart.

6. Hold up another sentence strip and read it aloud, together with the class:

> *We will play outside today.*

Ask students whether this is likely or unlikely. Then tape it on the Likely column. Continue this process using a variety of likely and unlikely sentences, such as the following:

> *The principal will come into our room today.*

An astronaut will come into our room today in his space suit.

We will learn how to fly an airplane today.

We will read books today.

Someone in our class will win a million dollars tomorrow.

We will go home after school today.

Playing the Game

1. Show the students two dice and ask, "When rolling two dice, which sums or answers are possible if you add the numbers on the dice together?" Brainstorm the sums with the class, recording all the possible sums (2–12) on the board.

2. Show the students an overhead transparency of the *Roll Two Dice* record sheet.

3. Write the following directions for the game on the board and model how to play the game, rolling just a few times to clarify the game without giving away the possible results.

  a. *Roll the dice.*
  b. *Add the numbers that come up.*
  c. *Write down the combination, or way to make the sum, in the box below the sum.*
  d. *Roll until one sum gets to the finish line.*

4. Before students begin playing the game, introduce the following sentence frame:

I predict that _____ will win.

5. Direct the students to use the frame to make predictions about which sum will win the race.

6. Hand out the materials and ask students to begin playing. When the students are about halfway through with the game, stop their play and have them revise their predictions by using the following sentence frames:

I predict that _____ *will win.*

I predict that _____ *will win because* _____ .

7. Have students continue to play until one sum wins the race.

8. Poll the students to determine which sum won for each game, and tally the results on the board. Ask the students what they notice about the data, then have them share their observations with their partners. Introduce the words *most* and *least* and ask the following questions:

   ✦ Which sums were rolled the most?
   ✦ Which sums were rolled the least?
   ✦ Which sum won the game?

✦ Roll Two Dice

Day 2

Writing About New Predictions

1. Return the *Roll Two Dice* record sheets to the students. Brainstorm with the class all of the possible ways to get each of the sums, 2–12, and record them underneath each sum on the board, for example:

2	3	4	5	6	7	8	9	10	11	12
1 + 1	1 + 2	2 + 2								
	2 + 1	1 + 3								
		3 + 1								

Ask students what they notice about this chart.

2. Ask the students to think about what they learned from the *Roll Two Dice* games in order to answer these questions:

✦ If we play *Roll Two Dice* again, which sum or sums are likely to win?
✦ Which sum or sums are unlikely to win?

3. Introduce the following sentence frames and have students draw conclusions and make new predictions in writing on the back of their record sheets:

If we play Roll Two Dice *again,* _____ *is likely to win.*

If we play Roll Two Dice *again,* _____ *is unlikely to win.*

If we play Roll Two Dice *again,* _____ *is likely to win because* _____ *.*

If we play Roll Two Dice *again,* _____ *is unlikely to win because* _____ *.*

4. To end the lesson, have a few volunteers read their writing to the class.

Building Iguanas with Pattern Blocks 6

An Algebra Lesson

Overview

This lesson gives students experience building, extending, and describing growth patterns. To begin, students compare and contrast patterns that repeat and patterns that grow. Then, the students are introduced to a "newborn iguana" built from pattern blocks. They predict what a one-year-old iguana might look like and then extend the pattern to three-year-old and four-year-old iguanas. They record the information on a chart, look for patterns, and extend the patterns to predict the number of blocks needed for ten-year-old and twenty-five-year-old iguanas.

Math Goal: Students will describe, extend, and make generalizations about growth patterns.

Language Goal: Students will compare and contrast and make predictions about patterns.

Key Vocabulary: body, changes, constant, feet, grows, head, one-year-old iguana, pattern, predict, tail, ten-year-old iguana, twenty-five-year-old iguana, variable, varies

Materials

✦ 15 word cards for key vocabulary terms
✦ 7 sentence strips or pieces of construction paper for sentence frames

- ✦ 1 set of overhead pattern blocks
- ✦ pattern blocks, 1 bucket or plastic sandwich bag per small group of students
- ✦ picture or photograph of an iguana
- ✦ optional: pocket chart

Sentence Frames That Help Students Compare and Contrast

Beginning

The _____ has _____.

The _____ is _____.

Intermediate

The _____ is/has _____, but the _____ is/has _____. Both have _____.

Advanced

While the _____ and the _____ both have _____, _____ _____.

Sentence Frames That Help Students Make Predictions

Beginning

I predict that the _____ will have _____.

Intermediate and Advanced

I predict that the _____ will have _____ because _____.

Class Profile

In Ms. Mendoza's class, there is a range of English language learners (ELLs). Some students are beginning English speakers, some are at the early intermediate level, and some are advanced speakers of English. Of the twenty-seven students in Ms. Mendoza's class, eight are native English speakers.

From the Classroom

✦ Building Iguanas, Day 1

Minilesson Introducing Academic Language

Kathy Melanese held up a card with the word *pattern* written on it and placed it in a pocket chart at the front of the room. She directed the students in Ms. Mendoza's class to read the word aloud with her, and asked the students to think about what came to mind when they heard the word *patterns*.

After a few seconds of think time, Kathy asked for students' ideas about patterns.

"It's like there's one shape and a different shape and it keeps going," Alex said.

"You can have a pattern like girl-boy-girl-boy-girl-boy," Amanda said.

"So you can have patterns that repeat?" Kathy asked. Amanda nodded in agreement.

"Talk with your neighbor about patterns that you see inside the classroom," Kathy directed.

The noise level in the room rose as students searched the classroom for patterns and shared ideas. Kathy did a quick lap around the room, listening in on students' conversations. As she passed by, she could hear Carmelo, an intermediate English speaker, sharing with Sarai, a beginning English speaker.

"There's a pattern on the wall," Carmelo said, motioning to the far side of the class. "The pattern is purple paper–yellow paper–purple paper–yellow."

Sarai responded, pointing to another wall in the classroom, "I see orange-yellow-orange-yellow on that wall over there."

After a minute or so, Kathy called the students back to attention and asked for ideas.

"I see a pattern in the American flag," Lilibeth noted. Ms. Mendoza's face lit up with a smile. Lilibeth is a beginning English speaker and is usually shy and quiet.

"Thumbs up if you noticed the pattern on the flag," Kathy directed. She wanted as many students participating as possible. "Lilibeth, can you tell us about the pattern that you see on the flag?"

"It repeats; it's like red-white-red, and it goes on like that," Lilibeth explained.

"Other patterns you noticed?" Kathy asked the class.

"There's a pattern on my clothes," Jackie shared. "It's a stripe pattern that goes over and over. It repeats."

After a few more students reported their ideas, Kathy told the class to observe and listen to the pattern she was about to make. With her hands and fingers, she produced a repeating pattern that went like this:

clap-snap-clap-snap-clap-snap . . .

Kathy urged the students to join in with her as she clapped and snapped. When she finally stopped, the students continued the pattern on their own.

"So you knew how to continue the pattern!" Kathy exclaimed, smiling.

"It keeps repeating!" Sal observed.

Kathy then produced a different clap-snap pattern:

clap-snap-clap-clap-snap-clap-clap-clap-snap . . .

As with the first clap-snap pattern, Kathy had the students produce this second pattern along with her. As they clapped and snapped, the students made comments.

"This pattern is different!" Gevlikin called out.

"It's growing! The claps keep getting more!" Sal commented.

"So how are the two patterns the same and how are they different?" Kathy asked. "Think for a second." Giving English language learners time to think before participating in a discussion helps them formulate ideas.

"The first pattern repeats the same thing over and over," Harold observed.

"And the second one is growing," Xenya added.

"What do you mean by *growing*?" Kathy probed, emphasizing the word.

"Like, the second one grows, 'cause each time you clap more," Xenya explained. "Like, you clap, then snap, but then you clap two times, and you keep adding one more clap each time."

"So there are patterns that *repeat* and patterns that also *grow*," Kathy summed up. As she said this, Kathy placed the word card *grows* in the pocket chart and had the students say the word aloud with her.

Next, Kathy drew the following patterns on the board, labeling them *First Pattern* and *Second Pattern*:

First Pattern

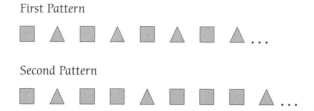

Second Pattern

After she finished drawing the two patterns, Kathy directed the class to read aloud each pattern, saying the names of each shape as she pointed to them. Then she introduced the following sentence frames and had the students read them aloud with her, pausing for the blank spaces:

The _____ has _____.

The _____ is _____.

The _____ is/has _____, but the _____ is/has _____. Both have _____.

While the _____ and the _____ both have _____, _____ _____.

Kathy had color-coded the frames pink for beginning, blue for intermediate, and green for advanced. Color-coding the sentence frames according to difficulty level makes it easier for students to differentiate between the frames. During a lesson, Kathy will sometimes suggest that a student use a particular frame that is more suited for him. Instead of having to say to a student, "I suggest that you use the frame for beginners," Kathy can refer to the frames by color and say something like, "Try the pink frame first."

After she introduced the frames, Kathy said to the class, "Let's practice comparing and contrasting the first pattern and the second pattern using one of the sentence frames." She prompted the class by reading the first part of the pink frame, the one most appropriate for beginning English speakers:

"The first pattern has . . . ," she read, pointing to the frame.

"The first pattern has squares and triangles!" Brianna exclaimed.

"The first pattern is . . . ," Kathy continued.

"The first pattern is repeating!" students called out in unison.

"What about the second pattern?" Kathy asked.

"The second pattern is growing," Amanda observed.

"The second pattern has more squares than triangles!" Jackie noted with enthusiasm.

"Who can compare the patterns using a different sentence frame?" Kathy asked. She waited a few seconds to give students some think time, then called on Lupita.

"The first pattern is repeating and the second pattern is growing," Lupita began, using the sentence frame for support. "Both have triangles and squares."

"I have one for the other sentence frame," Sal said. Looking up at the most advanced sentence frame for assistance, he continued, "While the first pattern and the second pattern both have squares, the second pattern grows."

After Sal finished sharing, Kathy gave the students a minute to practice comparing and contrasting the two patterns with a partner. Giving students time to practice using the sentence frames is an essential part of helping them develop their English language skills.

When conversations started to wind down, Kathy asked the class, "Can anyone else use the sentence frames to compare and contrast the patterns?"

"The first pattern has squares and triangles and the second pattern has more squares than triangles," Lilibeth said.

"The second pattern changes and the first pattern keeps staying the same," Fausto noticed.

After Fausto shared his observation, Kathy placed the word cards *changes* and *varies* in the pocket chart and, emphasizing the new vocabulary words, said, "Fausto told us that the second pattern *changes*. We can also say that the pattern *varies*."

Pointing to the words in the pocket chart, Kathy directed the class to say them aloud in a choral voice. Next, Kathy placed the word card *predict* in the pocket chart and asked if anyone knew what the word meant.

"It's like a guess," Brianna said.

"That's correct," Kathy responded. As she pointed to the first and second patterns on the board, she said, "We're going to *predict*, or guess, what shape the patterns will have next." She wrote a question mark at the end of each pattern to indicate what she meant by *predict*:

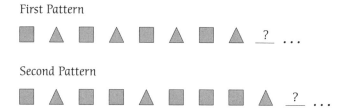

First Pattern

Second Pattern

Before students made their predictions, Kathy introduced the following sentence frames, which she labeled pink for beginning and green for intermediate and advanced, and had the students read them aloud, pausing for the blank spaces:

> I predict that the _____ will have _____.

> I predict that the _____ will have _____ because _____.

"What about the first pattern?" Kathy said. "What shape will the first pattern have next?"

"I predict the first pattern will have a square next," Freddy said.

"Thumbs up if you agree with Freddy," Kathy directed. Lots of students agreed.

"Other predictions?" Kathy asked.

"I predict that the first pattern will have a triangle next," Fausto said.

"What about Fausto's prediction? Who agrees with him?" Kathy asked. A few students motioned that they agreed.

After Kathy gave the students a minute or so to share their predictions about the first pattern with a partner, she asked the class about the second pattern.

"Square-square-square," Jackie guessed.

"Use the sentence frame to help you make your prediction," Kathy urged, wanting Jackie to use complete sentences.

"I predict the second pattern will be square-square-square," Jackie said. She altered the frame, using *will be* rather than *will have*. Kathy accepted this, knowing that the frames are there for support and should not restrict language production.

"I predict that the second pattern will have square-square-triangle," Maria Elena said. Maria Elena is a beginning English speaker. In fact, she is the student with the least experience with English in Ms. Mendoza's class. With the right support, students like Maria Elena can participate in whole-class discussions. Without the kind of scaffolding that sentence frames and vocabulary charts provide, these beginning speakers of English would most likely sit quietly and miss out on using language to clarify and further their math thinking.

"Other predictions?" Kathy prodded.

"I predict that the second pattern will have four squares because the pattern is growing and it's the square, then two squares, three squares, then four squares," Gevlikin reasoned, using the frame that prompted her to explain her thinking.

After students practiced making predictions with a partner, Kathy revealed the next shapes in both patterns by drawing them on the board:

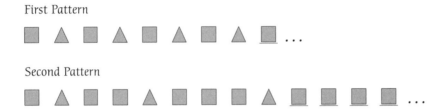

First Pattern

Second Pattern

Building Iguanas with Pattern Blocks

"We're now going to learn about and talk about some other patterns that grow," Kathy told the class. "In a minute or so, I'm going to make an iguana out of pattern blocks on the overhead projector. Raise your hand if you know what an iguana is." Many hands shot in the air.

To provide an opportunity for classroom conversations and to tap students' prior knowledge, Kathy gave the students about thirty seconds to talk at their tables about iguanas. As students shared, Kathy made a quick lap around the room. Following are some of the comments she heard:

"I have an iguana in my house like a pet!"

"I like iguanas!"

"My cousin has two iguanas."

"Iguanas go in trees."

"Iguanas are like little animals."

"Iguanas live in Mexico!"

"They're reptiles."

"They have long tails."

Kathy was impressed with the students' prior knowledge about iguanas. She quickly showed them a photograph of a real iguana from a resource book; the students were excited.

Next, Kathy placed the following transparent pattern blocks on the overhead projector: a hexagon, a square, a rhombus, and two triangles. As Kathy touched each shape, she asked the students to say the name aloud. It seemed that everyone in the class was familiar with the geometric shapes and their mathematical names. When all the shapes were introduced, Kathy used the pattern blocks to make a newborn iguana:

"This is a newborn iguana," Kathy began. She then touched each part of the iguana, telling the students that the hexagon was the body, the square was the head, the two triangles were the iguana's feet, and the rhombus was the tail. As she introduced the parts of the iguana, Kathy placed the following word cards in the pocket chart at the front of the room and had the students read them aloud: *body, head, feet,* and *tail.* Then, Kathy quickly sketched a picture of the newborn iguana on the chalkboard and labeled the parts. Again, she had the students say aloud the name of each part.

"I want you to *predict,* or guess, what a one-year-old iguana might look like," Kathy told the class. She held up a word card with *one-year-old iguana* written on it, placed it in the pocket chart, and asked the students to use the same sentence frames they previously used to help them make their predictions:

I predict that the _____ *will have* _____ .

I predict that the _____ *will have* _____ *because* _____ .

"I predict that it will have a longer tail," Harold guessed.

"I would use another hexagon," Esme added, not making use of the frames, but producing a grammatically correct prediction.

"I predict the newborn baby iguana will have two diamonds for the tail because it will grow one more tail," Amanda explained.

"You mean two *rhombi* for the tail?" Kathy asked, pushing for the correct mathematical name for the shape. Amanda nodded and repeated her prediction with the correction.

José, a beginning English speaker, used the sentence frame as a guide and said, "I predict it will have a big body." Kathy invited José to come up to the overhead and show the class what he meant using the overhead pattern blocks. As he added another hexagon for the body, he repeated his prediction, giving him another opportunity to practice his English language skills.

After giving students a few seconds to talk about their predictions with a partner, Kathy showed the class what a one-year-old iguana looked like by building it on the overhead projector and then drawing it next to the newborn iguana on the chalkboard:

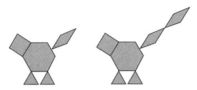

As Kathy pointed to the newborn and one-year-old iguanas, she asked the students to think about what was the same and what was different about them. Kathy directed the students to use any of the sentence frames they were introduced to earlier to help them compare and contrast the two iguanas.

"The only thing that changes is the tail," Amanda observed.

Kathy turned to the class and said, "Did you notice that Amanda used one of our vocabulary words, *changes*, to compare the two iguanas?"

Fausto, an advanced English speaker, said, "I don't think I'm using the sentence frames, but I think they have . . . what's different is the tail on the newborn. It has a little tail and the one-year-old iguana has two tails."

"Try using the green sentence frame [the most advanced frame] with your idea, Fausto," Kathy said. "While the . . . ," she prompted.

Making a second attempt, Fausto said, "While the newborn and the one-year-old both have tails, the one-year-old iguana has two tails."

Xenya, another advanced English speaker, said, "The one-year-old varies from the newborn because of its tail. It's changing."

"Xenya just used two new vocabulary words to describe how the iguanas are different: *changing* and *varies*," Kathy pointed out. "*Change* and *vary* can mean the same thing."

After Kathy provided time for students to practice comparing and contrasting the newborn and one-year-old iguanas with a partner, she asked students to predict what a two-year-old iguana would look like. Kathy reminded the students that they could use the sentence frames for support.

"I predict that the two-year-old iguana will have one more tail," Christian said.

"There's going to be a little triangle under the square and maybe another tail," Sylvia predicted.

Esme, an intermediate English speaker, said, "The baby will grow."

"How?" Kathy asked, pushing for more language.

Esme sat, thinking.

Kathy decided to ask a question to prompt Esme. "What part of the two-year-old will grow?"

Esme looked at the sentence frames and said, "I predict that the body will grow."

When students finished making predictions, Kathy built the two-year-old iguana on the overhead projector with transparent pattern blocks and sketched it on the board next to the newborn and one-year-old:

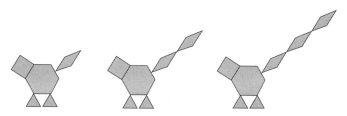

When Sal saw the three iguanas, he exclaimed, "It's a growing pattern! The newborn has one tail, the one-year-old has two tails, and the two-year-old has three tails."

"So what's *changing*? What *varies*?" Kathy asked the class as she pointed to each of the three iguanas drawn on the board.

"The tail!" students chorused.

"And what's staying the same?" Kathy asked.

"The body!" several students responded.

Kathy placed the word card *constant* in the pocket chart and explained to the students that *constant* means staying the same. She had the class say the word aloud with her. Then Kathy directed the class to complete her prompt: "In the pattern, the . . . [tail] changes or varies."

"In the pattern, the . . . [body] is constant or stays the same."

"But the head and the feet stay the same, too," Alex challenged.

"That's right," Kathy acknowledged, pointing to each part of the two-year-old iguana. She clarified, "From now on, we'll say that the head, body, and feet are called the body."

After students had discussed the newborn, one-year-old, and two-year-old iguanas, Kathy distributed pattern blocks to the students and directed them to build what they thought a three-year-old iguana would look like. When the students were finished, Kathy called on a volunteer to come up to the overhead and build a three-year-old iguana using transparent pattern blocks. Gio built the following figure:

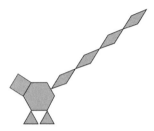

Kathy confirmed that Gio had correctly built the three-year-old. Most students had little difficulty making the three-year-old iguana. A few, however, had to make some adjustments. Kathy quickly sketched a three-year-old iguana on the board next to the newborn, one-year-old, and two-year-old.

To end the lesson for the day, Kathy asked the students to look at the iguanas, think about whether they noticed a pattern, and also think about the following questions:

- How is the pattern growing?
- What's staying the same or constant?
- What's changing, or what varies?
- How is the tail growing?

After the students identified the tail as growing by one each time and the body as remaining constant, Kathy directed the students to build a four-year-old iguana on their desk before collecting the pattern blocks. She told the students they'd be continuing their work with the pattern blocks the following day.

✦ Building Iguanas, Day 2

Charting the Iguana Pattern

Kathy began Day 2 of the lesson by showing the students a chart she had drawn on the board:

Years Old	Body + Tail	Total Number of Blocks

Pointing to the drawing of the newborn iguana on the board, Kathy posed the following questions to the students:

- ✦ How many blocks do we need for a newborn iguana's body?
- ✦ How many blocks do we need for a newborn iguana's tail?
- ✦ How many total blocks for the newborn iguana?

As students answered her questions, Kathy recorded the information on the chart. She asked the same questions for the one-year-old, two-year-old, three-year-old, and four-year-old iguanas. When she was finished, the chart looked like this:

Years Old	Body + Tail	Total Number of Blocks
newborn iguana	4 + 1	5
one-year-old iguana	4 + 2	6
two-year-old iguana	4 + 3	7
three-year-old iguana	4 + 4	8
four-year-old iguana	4 + 5	9

Pointing to the chart, Kathy asked the class, "What do you notice about the numbers under the column that says Body Plus Tail?" She provided a verbal prompt for the students: "The body . . ."

"The body keeps going four, four, four, four," Brianna, an advanced English speaker, observed.

Alex, an intermediate English speaker, added, "It's four all the way down."

"I notice it's staying the same," Sarah said.

"We can say the body is staying the *same* or *constant*," Kathy summed up as she wrote the word *Constant* above the word *Body* on the chart.

Building Iguanas with Pattern Blocks

"What do you notice about the tail numbers?" Kathy asked the class. Again, she provided a verbal prompt to support the students: "The tail numbers . . ."

"The tail numbers are going one, two, three," Freddy said.

"Yeah, it's adding one more each time," Jevrean said, building on Freddy's comment.

"The tail changes and goes up by one each time and the body always stays at four," Amanda observed.

"So we can say that the tail numbers *grow* or *vary*," Kathy told the class. Writing the word *Variable* above the word *Tail* on the chart, Kathy continued, "The tail number is the variable in our pattern." Kathy also added the *variable* word card to the pocket chart.

Years Old	Constant Variable Body + Tail	Total Number of Blocks
newborn iguana	4 + 1	5
one-year-old iguana	4 + 2	6
two-year-old iguana	4 + 3	7
three-year-old iguana	4 + 4	8
four-year-old iguana	4 + 5	9

Kathy kept asking the students questions to help them focus on the growing pattern. "What do you notice about the number of years old the iguana is and the number of blocks it takes to make the tail? Talk to a partner about what you notice."

This question was a crucial one in terms of how this particular growing pattern works. Knowing that the number of blocks in the tail is just one more than the iguana's age is key to being able to generalize the pattern; however, this wasn't obvious to most of the students. To help them focus on how the growing pattern worked, Kathy said, "Listen to this statement, and think about whether you agree or disagree: The number of blocks it takes to build the tail is one more than the iguana's age."

After a second or two, a few students raised their hands. Kathy didn't call on them, but waited; she wanted to restate the idea using different wording. Rephrasing can give English learners another chance to make sense of an idea.

Kathy continued, pointing to the chart, "Take the iguana's age and add one. That will tell you how many blocks for the tail." This prompted a greater response from students, and many more hands were now raised. Kathy called on Gio.

"When you told us to build a three-year-old iguana, we used four for the tail," he said.

"Look," Sal stated emphatically. "You have a two-year-old iguana and it has three for the tail, and a four-year-old iguana and it has five for the tail. It's always the age and one more to make the tail."

"And I see that to get the total number of blocks, you take the body and add the number of blocks for the tail and you get the total blocks," Jessica explained.

"So let's think about how many total blocks you would need for a five-year-old iguana," Kathy said to the class. "How many for the body?"

"Four!" students responded.

"Will the body always have four blocks, no matter how old the iguana is?" Kathy probed. She pointed to the chart and the column with the numbers that represented the iguanas' bodies.

"The body will always be made of four blocks, 'cause on the chart, every iguana has four for the body," Harold explained.

"Nod your head if you agree," Kathy told the class. She wanted to be sure that the students understood this part of the pattern. "Now, how many blocks for the tail on a five-year-old? Sal said it's always one more than the age of the iguana. So how much is one more than five?"

Kathy let the students think for a minute or so about her question and then directed the students to think about the total number of blocks needed for a five-year-old iguana. When everyone seemed to agree that it would take ten blocks, Kathy posed two problems for the students to solve.

As she held up the two word cards with *ten-year-old iguana* and *twenty-five-year-old-iguana* written on them, Kathy posed the problems. "I'm going to hand out some paper, and I want you to use words, numbers, and/or pictures to figure out how many total blocks it will take to build a ten-year-old iguana," she instructed, speaking slowly and enunciating each word. "And since iguanas can live to be about twenty-five years old, I want you to try to figure out how many total blocks it would take to build a twenty-five-year-old."

When Kathy was confident that everyone understood the directions, she distributed paper and students began to work. Kathy encouraged the students to use the sentence frames they'd learned in the lesson to help them.

Observing the Students

As Kathy circulated, she noticed that some students were immediately able to solve the problem for a ten-year-old iguana and moved on to

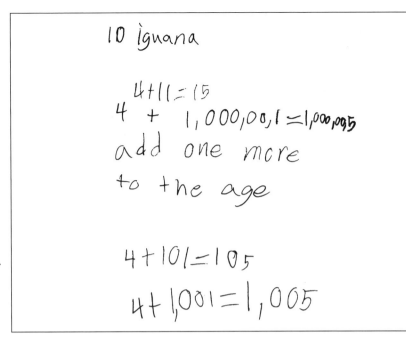

FIGURE 6-1.
Harold chal-
lenged him-
self to work
with large
numbers.

figuring the number of blocks needed for a twenty-five-year-old iguana
and even for a one hundred–year-old! Other students struggled to figure out how the pattern worked and resorted to drawing pictures or
re-creating the chart.

Harold, a native English speaker, quickly figured out the answer
for a ten-year-old iguana. He then challenged himself and found out
how many total blocks it would take to build a hundred-year-old and
a million-year-old iguana. (See Figure 6–1.)

Esme, an early intermediate English speaker, re-created the chart
to help her figure the answers. She quickly noticed how the pattern
worked and was able to predict the total number of blocks needed for
a twenty-five-year-old, a hundred-year-old, and a thousand-year-old
iguana. (See Figure 6–2.)

José, a beginning English speaker, struggled at first to figure out
how the pattern worked. He seemed to have little experience with reading charts and identifying patterns. However, he used drawings to help
him find the answer for a ten-year-old iguana. Although he didn't
explain his reasoning on paper, he used a sentence frame to tell Kathy
about his prediction: "I predict that the ten-year-old iguana will have
sixteen blocks." (See Figure 6–3.)

Sal, a native English speaker, explained his reasoning: *I used the
age and added one more to the block on the tail.* He successfully figured

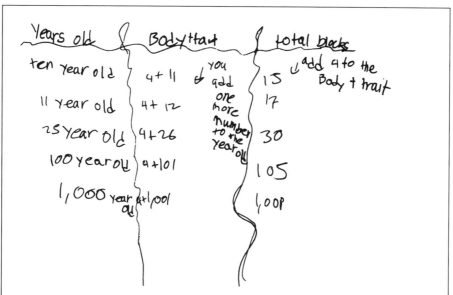

Years old	Body+tail	total blocks
ten year old	4 + 11	you add one more number to the year old 15 add 4 to the Body + trait
11 year old	4 + 12	17
25 year old	4 + 26	30
100 year old	4 + 101	105
1,000 year old	4 + 1001	1,008

FIGURE 6-2.
Esme solved
the problem
for five
iguanas.

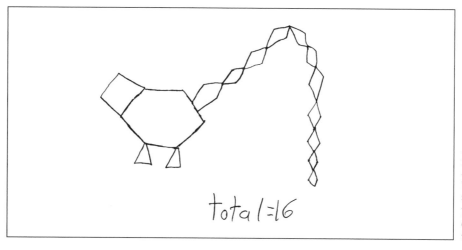

total = 16

FIGURE 6-3.
José used a
picture to
solve the
problem but
counted
incorrectly.

out the total number of blocks for a twenty-five-year-old and a hundred-year-old iguana. (See Figure 6–4.)

Brianna, an advanced English speaker, explained how the pattern worked: *I now because there is always 1 more than the age.* (See Figure 6–5.)

Learning how to describe, extend, and make generalizations about patterns takes time and experience. As they develop their algebraic thinking, all students benefit from seeing patterns represented in multiple ways: with concrete objects like pattern blocks, with pictures, with numbers, and with words.

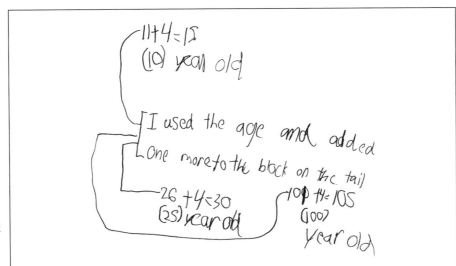

FIGURE 6-4.
Sal solved
three iguana
problems and
explained
how he
figured.

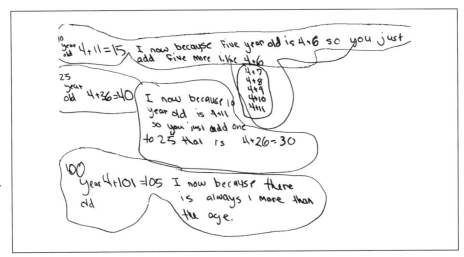

FIGURE 6-5.
Brianna
explained
how she
solved each
problem.

Using language to think, discuss, and reflect helps students unlock the mysteries of algebra. When the students in Ms. Mendoza's class were able to articulate how the iguana was growing, it helped them to predict, without physical evidence, how many blocks it would take to build older iguanas. The challenge for teachers is to learn how to support students who are using the English language to describe patterns when, at the same time, they are learning how to speak English. The strategies that Kathy used in the lesson are examples of the kind of support that ELLs need.

Activity Directions ✦ **Building Iguanas with Pattern Blocks**

Day 1

Minilesson Introducing Academic Language

1. Place the word card *pattern* on the vocabulary chart. Ask students what they know about patterns. Have the class share their ideas and then provide several examples of both repeating and growing patterns. Have students extend each pattern and talk about whether it repeats or grows, and how each growth pattern is growing. Place the word card *grows* on the vocabulary chart.

2. On the board, draw two patterns:

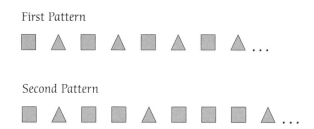

First Pattern

Second Pattern

Ask the students what they notice about the two patterns and have them compare and contrast the patterns. Introduce the following sentence frames to help students talk about the two patterns. Ask the students to practice the frames, pausing for the blank spaces.

Beginning

> *The _____ has _____.*

> *The _____ is _____.*

Intermediate

> *The _____ is/has _____, but the _____ is/has _____. Both have _____.*

Advanced

> *While the* _____ *and the* _____ *both have*
> _____, _____ _____.

Have students share with a partner, using the sentence frames to compare the two patterns. When they've finished, have students share with the class. Look for students to use the words *grow*, *growing*, *change*, *changes*, *vary*, *varies* (or similar words) to describe the growing pattern. If they don't use them, introduce the vocabulary words and place word cards for *changes* and *varies* on the vocabulary chart.

3. Ask students if they know what it means to *predict* or make a *prediction*. Place the word card *predict* on the vocabulary chart, tell the students that it's like a guess, and provide some examples.

4. Ask the students to predict what shape will come next in the repeating pattern and the growing pattern. Introduce the following sentence frames to help students make predictions. Ask the students to practice the frames, pausing for the blank spaces.

Beginning

> *I predict that the* _____ *will have* _____.

Intermediate/Advanced

> *I predict that the* _____ *will have* _____ *because* _____.

Have the students share their predictions with a partner, using the sentence frames. When they're finished, have them share with the class. Then reveal what shapes come next in both patterns and draw them on the board.

Building Iguanas with Pattern Blocks

1. Tell students that for this lesson, they'll be learning about patterns that grow. First, they'll need to use their imagination to try to figure out the growing pattern you have in mind. Tell them you are going to make a baby iguana with pattern blocks on the overhead. Ask students if

they know what an iguana is and have a brief conversation. Build the newborn iguana on the overhead.

2. Go over the parts of the baby iguana—head, body, feet, and tail—and place the corresponding word cards on the vocabulary chart. Draw a picture of the newborn iguana on the board.

3. Ask students to think about what a one-year-old iguana might look like. Show them a word card with *one-year-old iguana* written on it. Have the students use the prediction sentence frames introduced earlier to share their predictions with a partner. Then have them share their ideas with the class.

4. Show students what a one-year-old iguana looks like using overhead pattern blocks, and sketch the one-year-old next to the newborn on the board.

5. Ask students to examine the newborn and one-year-old and tell you what's the same and what's different about them. Have the students use the compare and contrast sentence frames introduced earlier to talk about the two iguanas.

    Have students share their thinking with a partner, then have them share their ideas with the class.

6. Next, have students predict what a two-year-old iguana will look like. Have students use the same sentence frames that they used to predict for a one-year-old iguana. Have students do a think, pair, share, then share their ideas with the class. After students share, show them what a two-year-old iguana looks like on the overhead and draw a picture of it on the board.

7. Ask the students to look at the newborn, the one-year-old, and the two-year-old. Ask them if they notice a *pattern*. Ask the students how the pattern is *growing*. Ask the students what *changes* or *varies* (the tail) and what stays the *same* or what is *constant* (the body). Place the word *constant* on the vocabulary chart.

    After students identify that the body of the iguana stays the same and the tail changes, prompt the class to use words to describe the pattern. For example, say, "In the pattern, the . . . changes," or "In the pattern, the . . . stays the same."

8. Next, distribute pattern blocks and direct students to build a three-year-old iguana on their desk with the blocks. When they are finished, have a volunteer come up to the overhead and build a three-year-old iguana.

Draw a picture of the three-year-old on the board next to the other iguanas. Ask the class to look at the pattern. Again, ask:

- How is the pattern growing?
- What's staying the same or constant?
- What's changing, or what varies?
- How is the tail growing? (It increases or gets bigger by one each time)

9. Direct students to build a four-year-old iguana on their desk, then collect the materials.

Day 2

1. Draw a chart on the board that looks like this:

Years Old	Body + Tail	Total Number of Blocks

Refer to the drawing of the newborn iguana on the board and ask students:

- How many blocks do we need for a newborn iguana's body?
- How many blocks do we need for a newborn iguana's tail?
- How many total blocks do we for the newborn iguana?

As students answer your questions, record the information on the chart. Continue asking the same questions for the one-year-old, two-year-old, three-year-old, and four-year-old iguanas and record the information as students provide it.

2. Ask the students: "What do you notice about the numbers under the column that says Body Plus Tail?" Point to the column on the chart as you ask this question.

Provide a verbal prompt for students: "The body . . ." Possible responses:

- The body always stays the same.
- The four goes on and on.

Say to the students: "Mathematicians say that when something stays the same, it is constant." Point to the word *constant* on the vocabulary chart. On the pattern chart, write *Constant* above *Body*.

Provide students with a few examples of the word *constant* in sentences.

3. Ask the students: "What do you notice about the tail numbers?" Provide a verbal prompt for students: "The tail numbers . . ." Possible responses:

- The tail numbers change.
- The tail numbers go up by one.
- The tail numbers add one each time.
- The tail numbers get bigger.

Say to the students: "Numbers like the tail numbers that change, or vary, are the *variable* part of the pattern." Point to the word *varies* on the vocabulary chart and add the word card *variable* to the vocabulary chart. Write the word *Variable* on the pattern chart above *Tail*.

4. You might ask students: "What do you notice about the number of years old the iguana is and the number of blocks it takes to make its tail?" If no one offers the pattern, tell students that the number of blocks in the tail is one more than the number of years.

5. Ask the students to think about how many *total blocks* you would need to build a five-year-old iguana. Give them a minute or two to figure it out, then ask for ideas.

Point to the two-column chart and ask: "How many blocks for the body on a five-year-old iguana? How do you know? How many blocks for the tail? How do you know? How many blocks total? How do you know?"

6. Hand out paper and ask the students to use words, pictures, and/or numbers to answer two questions: "How many total blocks will you need to build a ten-year-old iguana? How many total blocks will you need to build a twenty-five-year-old iguana?" Have students use the

prediction sentence frames to support them in making their predictions. Show them the word cards *ten-year-old iguana* and *twenty-five-year-old iguana.*

7. Observe students as they work and provide assistance as needed.

8. If there's time, you could pose a challenge: "What if iguanas lived to be one hundred? How many blocks would you need to build a hundred-year-old iguana?"

Round Things 7

A Measurement Lesson

Overview

In this lesson, students measure the diameter and circumference of different circular objects, record the measurements, and then compare them to discover the relationship between the circumference and the diameter of circles (also known as *pi*, or 3.14).

In a minilesson prior to the lesson, students are introduced to the vocabulary words and sentence frames that they will need in order to compare two numbers or measurements. The remainder of the vocabulary words are introduced throughout the lesson as the need arises.

Math Goal: Students will compare the circumferences of circles with their diameters and draw conclusions about the relationship between the two measurements.

Language Goal: Students will compare and contrast and draw conclusions.

Key Vocabulary: about/around/approximately, bigger, division/divide, longer, multiplication/multiply, shorter, the circumference, the diameter, the radius, smaller, $\frac{1}{2}, \frac{1}{3}, \frac{1}{4}, \frac{1}{5}$

Materials

- ✦ 1 sheet of chart paper for key vocabulary terms
- ✦ 3 different-colored markers (e.g. green, blue, and red)
- ✦ a variety of circular objects (soda can, coffee can, plastic cup, lids to containers, etc., which students should be asked to bring to class), 5 per pair of students
- ✦ 2-foot pieces of string, 5 per pair of students

+ rulers or tape measures, 1 per pair of students
+ white construction paper, 1 sheet per pair of students
+ enlarged version of *Round Things* record sheet written on a piece of chart paper (see Blackline Masters)
+ *Round Things* record sheets, 1 per student
+ 2 or 3 construction paper circles with differing circumferences

Sentence Frames That Help Students Make Comparisons

Beginning

| _____ is _____. _____ is _____. |

Intermediate

| _____ is _____ than _____. |

| _____ is _____ times _____ than _____. |

| _____ is _____ of _____. |

Advanced

| _____ is about/around/approximately _____ of _____. |

| _____ is about/around/approximately _____ times _____ than _____. |

Class Profile

In Janet Brown's class, there are thirty students; six are English language learners who are classified by the school's English learner program as reclassified fluent English proficient (RFEP), five are advanced speakers of English, and five are intermediate speakers of English. The remaining students are either native English speakers or ones that were initially identified as fluent English proficient (IFEP) students.

From the Classroom ◆ **Round Things, Day 1**

Minilesson Introducing Academic Language

Kathy Melanese tapped the prior knowledge of students in Janet Brown's class by asking them to think of a time when they had compared two different things. The students thought for a while and then chatted with their table groups. Conversations included comparisons of brothers and sisters, the size of cookies, and other familiar things in their lives.

"While I was circulating around the room, I heard lots of ideas about things that you've compared," Kathy said after she regained the students' attention. "Today, we're going to be comparing things as well. We'll start by having you compare two line segments."

Kathy then drew two line segments on the board and labeled them *A* and *B*:

String A
String B

"Let's pretend that these two line segments are pieces of string," Kathy told the class. "I want you to look at the pieces of string and compare them. Think about it for a few seconds, and then share your ideas with a partner." Giving students time to talk with a partner or in small groups is essential when teaching English language learners. Sometimes, ELLs are reluctant to risk speaking English in front of the whole class. Smaller groups provide opportunities to practice language and a safer environment in which to share ideas.

Kathy clapped twice to regain the students' attention and then elicited ideas from the class. Manuel is the student with the least experience with English in Janet's class, and he doesn't routinely share during whole-class discussions. Partner talk gave him time to rehearse expressing his thoughts.

"String A is bigger than String B," Manuel stated.

"String B is smaller than String A," Kay said.

"One is long, one is short," Corina added. According to her teacher, Corina is a student who struggles with both English *and* Spanish, her native language. Corina has difficulty using comparatives (*-er* as in *bigger*) and superlatives (*-est* as in *biggest*). Because comparing things was such an important part of this lesson, Kathy was aware that Corina might need extra support. She knew that Corina might also need some additional practice with comparatives and superlatives beyond the math lesson.

Sanjana, who was recently reclassified by the school's English learner program and is now an RFEP student, added, "String B is one-half and String A is a whole."

"How could we prove Sanjana's idea that String B is half of String A?" Kathy asked.

"We could measure it," Randall offered.

"If we could fold String A in half, we could compare it to String B to see if String B is half," Jay reasoned. Jay is a native English speaker and a strong math student.

"Or we could use our fingers to be String B and put it next to String A," Alfreda suggested. Kathy asked Alfreda to come up and demonstrate.

Alfreda used her thumb and index finger to measure the length of String B. Then she proceeded to take that length and iterate, or repeat, it next to String A. It took about two String B lengths to make String A.

"So String A *is two times longer* than String B," Kathy stated, modeling language that students would use in the upcoming lesson. She then drew two more line segments on the board, labeling these strings C and D:

After asking students to compare String C and String D, she waited about thirty seconds to give everyone lots of time to think. Wait time provides all students, especially English language learners, a chance to formulate their ideas and construct thoughts in English.

When Kathy thought she'd given students enough time, she called on Sara.

"I think String D is smaller than String C," she began. "String D looks like a third . . ."

"A third of . . . ," Kathy prompted.

"String D looks like a third of String C," Sara concluded.

"What made you think that?" Kathy asked. Sara looked a little bewildered, so Kathy called on Steven, another English learner, to come to the board and share his idea.

"Can I use a ruler?" Steven asked. Kathy obliged, handing him a ruler while commenting to the class that using measurement tools can be useful when comparing lengths.

Steven used the ruler to measure String D (about 3 inches in length) and then took the ruler and placed it next to String C. Steven iterated the 3-inch length four times until it matched the length of String C.

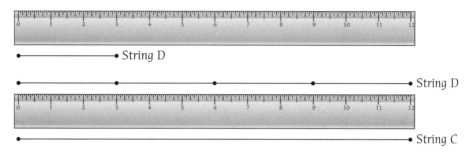

"So it takes four String Ds to make String C," Kathy stated. "Can anyone say that in a different way?"

"String C is four times longer than String D," Daisy said.

"So I've heard many of you use different words when comparing the strings," Kathy said as she taped to the board a large piece of white chart paper. On the chart were the three intermediate sentence frames, written in blue marker, and a place for vocabulary words. Kathy wrote the words *longer, shorter, bigger,* and *smaller* on the chart, as well as the fractions $\frac{1}{2}$, $\frac{1}{3}$, and $\frac{1}{4}$.

"I heard you use the words *longer* and *shorter*, *bigger* and *smaller*, and the fractions *one-half*, *one-third*, and *one-fourth* to describe and compare the strings," Kathy said, pointing to the words and fractions she had just written. She then introduced the following sentence frames, which were designed for intermediate-level English speakers.

> _____ is _____ than _____.

> _____ is _____ times _____ than _____.

> _____ is _____ of _____.

Because there were no beginning-level English learners in the class, Kathy chose not to introduce sentence frames for beginners. If a student required a more basic sentence frame during the lesson, Kathy had the following frame, written in green marker, ready to use:

> _____ is _____. _____ is _____.

"Can someone use one of the sentence frames to compare String C and String D?" Kathy asked. After a few seconds, she called on Estrellita.

"String C is four times bigger than String D," Estrellita said.

"What about another frame?" Kathy asked.

"String D is four times shorter than String C," Mea offered.

"String D is one-fourth of String C," Jay added.

Using the most basic frame, Fidel, an intermediate English speaker, said, "C is longer than D."

When students were finished sharing ideas, Kathy continued. "Next, we're going to compare numbers rather than line segments or string." On the board, she wrote the numbers *5* and *25* and asked the students to first think about how the numbers compared and then share their thinking with their partners. After about thirty seconds, Kathy called on Sara.

"Five times five is twenty-five, and twenty-five divided by five is five," Sara reported.

"So you can use multiplication and division to compare the numbers," Kathy acknowledged, writing the words *multiplication/multiply* and *division/divide* on the class chart. "Sara, can you use one of the sentence frames and the information you gave us to compare five and twenty-five?"

Sara thought for a few moments. Kathy recognized that she needed some help, so Kathy pointed to the middle sentence frame to get Sara started.

"Twenty-five is five times bigger than five," Sara said.

After Sara shared, Kathy had everyone in the class practice using the sentence frame by repeating Sara's idea together.

"Can anyone use this frame to compare five and twenty-five?" Kathy asked, pointing to the last sentence frame.

"Five is one-fifth of twenty-five," Brandy said.

"Good. That's a different fraction than we used before," Kathy pointed out as she added $\frac{1}{5}$ to the vocabulary chart. As with Sara's idea, Kathy had the class practice restating Brandy's idea using the sentence frame, pointing to each word as students read them aloud in unison. Explicit practice using the sentence frames is important if students are to use them effectively on their own during the lesson.

"Now I'm going to give you two different numbers that might be a challenge," Kathy told the class. On the board, she wrote $20\frac{1}{2}$ and *45*. She gave students about thirty seconds to talk at their tables, encouraging them to use the sentence frames when comparing the numbers.

As students discussed the numbers, Kathy circulated, listening in on their conversations. She noticed that students were having a difficult time comparing $20\frac{1}{2}$ and 45. They didn't seem sure how to explain what they thought because this new problem didn't fit easily into the previously shared frames. The students seemed to be in a verbal predicament.

When the talking died down, Kathy asked, "What made this more challenging?"

"Twenty and one-half doesn't go into forty-five evenly," May explained. "It doesn't divide evenly. Plus, it has a fraction; that's hard."

"I agree," Kathy said. "These numbers aren't as friendly as five and twenty-five."

Kathy then wrote two more sentence frames on the chart underneath the other three frames. She wrote these more advanced frames in red rather than in blue and had the students read them aloud, pausing for the blank spaces:

> _____ *is about/around/approximately* _____ *of*
> _____ .

> _____ *is about/around/approximately* _____
> *times* _____ *than* _____ .

"We use the words *about*, *around*, and *approximately* when we're estimating," Kathy told the class. "Sometimes we don't need to be exact or right on when measuring or calculating, just as long as we're close. Who thinks you can use one of the new sentence frames to compare twenty and one-half and forty-five?"

Kathy knew that comparing numbers would be more difficult than comparing string lengths. The visuals provided by the string lengths helped students use language to compare. Kathy hoped that students' experience comparing the strings would give them a foundation of understanding upon which to build.

Jorge, an intermediate English speaker, raised his hand hesitantly and explained, "I think that twenty and a half is around two times smaller than forty-five."

Kathy was impressed with Jorge's idea. The sentence frame certainly helped Jorge explain his math thinking, thereby providing a window into his number sense.

"Can you explain how you know that?" Kathy probed. Her question was met with silence, so she took another tack and asked the students how they could check Jorge's idea.

Evita, an advanced English speaker, explained, "If you add twenty and twenty it's forty, and a half plus a half is one, so it's forty-one. And forty-one is close to forty-five."

"Can someone retell what Evita just said in a different way?" Kathy asked the class. Having students rephrase other students' ideas serves two purposes: it gives everyone another chance to hear and make sense of the idea, and it pushes students to describe ideas in different ways. If you can say it in your own words, you own it.

"Twenty and a half times two is forty-one, 'cause twenty times two is forty and a half times a half is one, so it's forty-one," Jay explained.

"Twenty and a half is approximately one-half of forty-five," Paco offered, using the sentence frame for support.

After the class practiced comparing $20\frac{1}{2}$ and 45 using the sentence frames, Kathy moved onto *Round Things*, a measurement lesson.

Introducing the Lesson

To begin the measurement lesson, Kathy asked the students what they knew about circles. Although she knew that the students had some recent experience learning about circles, Kathy wanted them to review what they knew. Activating prior knowledge is important when teaching English language learners. Prior knowledge provides the foundation for interpreting new information, and it enables students to make inferences about the meaning of words and expressions that they may not have come across before.

Paco, an English learner with advanced proficiency, responded, "They are round." Paco's comment drew a few giggles from students, perhaps because they perceived his contribution as basic and obvious. Kathy intervened and reminded the class about the importance of respecting everyone's ideas. She knows that creating a safe environment is essential if English learners are to take risks and share their thinking.

Emmanuel added, "Circles don't have sides or corners."

"Circles are three hundred and sixty degrees," Jay said.

"They're closed figures," Brandy shared.

"You can measure the diameter and the radius," Kay offered.

Kathy added *the diameter* and *the radius* to the class chart. "What is the diameter and the radius?" Kathy queried. Kay shook her head, indicating that she didn't know. Sometimes students learn vocabulary in a rote manner, without connecting the words to something concrete or familiar. Kathy used this as a teaching opportunity, drawing a circle

FIGURE 7-1. The class chart for *Round Things.*

on the class chart. The chart now included the circle, the sentence frames, and the vocabulary bank. (See Figure 7–1.)

"Who can come up and show and tell where the diameter is on the circle I drew?" Kathy asked the class.

Estrellita walked to the board and used her finger to show a diameter on the circle. When she was finished, Kathy drew in the diameter and labeled it:

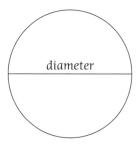

"Mathematicians say that the diameter is a line segment that passes across a circle through its center," Kathy told the class, speaking slowly and enunciating each word as she traced the diameter with her index finger. "Who can come up and show and tell where the radius is?"

Paco walked up to the board and traced the radius with his finger, saying, "The radius is from the center to the outside of the circle."

"And," Kathy added, "it's important to note that the radius is a line segment joining the center of a circle with any point on its circumference." With her finger, Kathy drew imaginary lines representing different radii on the circle. Then, as with the diameter, Kathy drew in and labeled a radius on the circle.

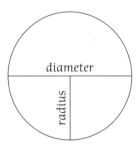

Next, she wrote *circumference* next to the circle drawn on the class chart and had the students say the word aloud with her.

"Think about whether you know where the circumference is on the circle," Kathy said.

After a few seconds, she called on Alan, who explained, "The circumference is the measurement around the circle."

Kathy traced the circumference of the circle with her finger and had the students say the word aloud with her. "*Circumference* starts like the word *circle*, with the letter C," She told the class. She then had the students use their index fingers to trace circles in the air while they repeated the word aloud.

Before introducing the measurement task to the class, Kathy wanted to make sure that students had a good understanding of the terminology presented: *diameter*, *radius*, and *circumference*. So she asked students to talk at their tables and explain to one another the meaning of the measurement words. As she circulated, Kathy noticed that most students understood the meaning of the vocabulary. However, there were two students at one table that were still confused.

Corina, an intermediate English speaker, and Cassandra, a native English speaker, both described the diameter as "half a circle," and the radius as "a fourth of a circle." After listening to the girls, Kathy realized that the circle she had drawn on the class chart was confusing the students. The circle was divided into two parts by the diameter, so the girls interpreted the diameter as being one half of the circle. Similarly, the radius on Kathy's drawing of the circle looked as if it divided one half of the circle into two equal parts, or fourths, so the girls thought that the radius meant one-fourth of the circle.

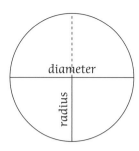

After Kathy offered a brief explanation, Corina and Cassandra seemed to have resolved their misconception. As Kathy moved onto another table, she reflected on Corina and Cassandra's dilemma. She was reminded that visuals can be powerful tools to help all students, especially English language learners, understand concepts and the vocabulary used to describe those concepts. At the same time, visuals can also confuse students, and teachers must be aware of this and constantly check in with students to find out how they perceive the important ideas being presented.

Next, Kathy introduced the measurement task. She began by explaining that students would be working in pairs and measuring the diameters and the circumferences of several circular objects that she had brought into the class. She held up a soda can for everyone to see.

"On the bottom of this soda can is a circle," Kathy said. She held up a piece of string and asked, "How could I use this string to measure the circumference and the diameter of the circle? Talk to a partner."

After a few seconds, Jessica volunteered to come up and demonstrate. She wrapped the string around the soda can, pinching it to show the circumference measurement. Her measurement was a little off because the string was overlapping a bit.

"Are you sure your measurement is accurate?" Kathy asked.

"What does *accurate* mean?" Paco asked, looking confused.

Kathy pointed to the red sentence frames, which included the words *about/around/approximately*. "We use these words when our measurements are estimates, not accurate ones," Kathy explained. "Accurate measurements are ones that we are very careful about. Jessica, wrap the string around the soda can again and be careful that the string doesn't overlap. This way, when you measure the circumference length, the measurement will be *accurate*."

After Jessica finished modeling how to find the circumference and diameter of the soda can using the string, cut the length of each with scissors, and measure each with a ruler, Kathy used an enlarged version of the *Round Things* record sheet to show the students how to record the diameter and circumference measurements. She also showed them how to tape the string lengths onto construction paper and label them:

Round Things		
Object	Diameter	Circumference
1. Soda can	$2\frac{1}{4}$"	$6\frac{1}{2}$"
2.		
3.		
4.		
5.		

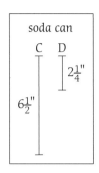

Before distributing supplies, Kathy asked the class to think about what unit of measurement to use. "Should you use miles? Yards? Inches? Centimeters?" She asked, offering a variety of units to get students thinking. "What do you think?"

"Inches."

"Centimeters."

"Both make sense to me," Kathy said. "But whatever unit you use to measure the circumference, you need to use the same unit to measure the diameter. That way, you'll be able to compare the two."

Kathy then chose volunteers to distribute circular objects, string, rulers, construction paper, tape, scissors, and *Round Things* record sheets. The students were eager to get to work.

Observing the Students

Once supplies were in students' hands, everyone seemed to be fully engaged. As they worked, Kathy circulated, listening in on students' conversations, asking questions, and lending a hand when needed.

Kathy sat down with Arie, an intermediate speaker of English, and Jorge, an advanced English speaker. "What are you measuring first?" Kathy asked.

"Can," Arie replied.

"A can of what?" Kathy asked, pushing for more language and a complete sentence.

"A can of soup. We're measuring the can of soup," Arie said.

Arie took the string and wrapped it around the can of soup. Kathy asked her which part she was measuring.

"It's the circumference," Arie responded.

After Arie wrote down the measurements on her record sheet, Kathy turned to Jorge. "Jorge, Arie just measured the circumference. Which part are you going to measure?"

Jorge looked puzzled. Using his finger, he pointed to the diameter of the circle on the soup can, but was at a loss as to the name. Kathy urged him to go up to the class chart and point to the part of the circle he would be measuring. Jorge walked up to the chart and found the label that read *diameter*. The vocabulary chart with the drawing of the circle proved to be a useful resource.

Once Jorge had measured the diameter using the string and had recorded the circumference and diameter measurements, Kathy asked him to compare the diameter and the circumference. Jorge took the string length that measured the circumference and taped it onto a piece of construction paper. He then took the string length that measured the diameter and compared it with the circumference length. It took about three diameter lengths to equal the circumference length:

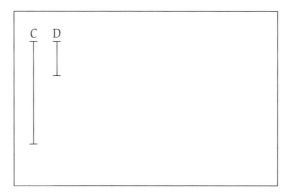

"The diameter is three times smaller," Jorge reported.

"Three times smaller than . . . ," Kathy prompted.

Jorge looked up at the blue sentence frames and said, "The diameter is three times smaller than the circumference."

Kathy picked up the tennis ball can on the table and asked Jorge and Arie to make a prediction about the relationship between the can's diameter and its circumference. "How do you think the diameter and the circumference of this can will compare?" Kathy asked them.

"It's going to be one-half as big," Jorge predicted.

"What's going to be one-half as big?" Kathy prodded.

"The diameter," Jorge responded, now identifying the name without looking at the vocabulary chart.

"The diameter is going to be . . . ," Kathy prompted.

"The diameter is going to be one-half as big as the circumference," Jorge said.

"Do you agree with Jorge?" Kathy asked Arie. She nodded in agreement.

Kathy did not want to press Jorge and Arie about their incorrect predictions just yet. Rather, she wanted them to test out their hypothesis and see if further experience would change their thinking.

After about fifteen minutes, math time came to a close for the day. Kathy told the students that they would finish measuring the circles the following day.

✦ Round Things, Day 2

A Class Discussion

Students resumed their work measuring the circumferences and diameters of the round things at their desks; Kathy gave them about fifteen minutes to finish up.

Before starting a class discussion, Kathy had a few volunteers collect the circular objects, scissors, rulers, string, and tape so that students wouldn't be distracted. Once everything was collected and put away, Kathy started with a question.

"I want each of you to look at the construction paper that has your string lengths," she directed. "What do you notice when you compare the circumference lengths and the diameter lengths?" Kathy gave the students several seconds to check out the string lengths and to digest the question she had posed. For example, one pair's paper looked like this:

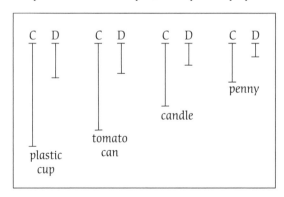

When students were ready, Kathy asked again, "So what do you notice?"

"The diameter is always smaller than the circumference," Alan observed.

"The diameter is about one-half or one-third of the circumference," Jay said.

No other hands were raised, so Kathy waited.

Looking at the sentence frames, May, an advanced English speaker, said, "The circumference is about three times longer than the diameter."

"How do you know that the circumference is three times longer than the diameter?" Kathy asked, pointing to the circumference and the diameter on the circle drawn on the class chart.

"I did the diameter times three," Angelita said. Several students nodded their heads in agreement.

"Did anyone do anything with your fingers to compare the diameter and the circumference lengths?" Kathy asked the class. Several students raised their hands.

Kathy positioned two strings next to one another on the overhead projector—one was the circumference length and one was the diameter length of a circle. She asked Emmanuel to come up and show how he used his fingers to measure the length of the circumference by iterating the diameter length three times.

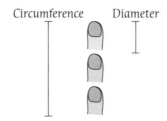

When Emmanuel was finished, Kathy directed the students to compare the string lengths on their construction paper using Emmanuel's method. Practicing this kinesthetic method gave students another chance to make sense of the mathematical relationship.

"Yeah, it takes three diameters to make a circumference!" Tammy exclaimed. Others agreed.

Next, Kathy elicited from students a sampling of the measurements from their *Round Things* record sheets. Following are the measurements she collected:

Object	Diameter	Circumference
lid	$6\frac{1}{2}$ cm	22 cm
container	11 cm	33 cm
lid	$2\frac{1}{2}$ in.	$8\frac{1}{2}$ in.
tennis ball lid	3 in.	$9\frac{1}{2}$ in.
can of peas	7 cm	21 cm

"Let's take a look at the number measurements," Kathy told the class. "How do the diameters and circumferences compare?" Kathy gave the students a few minutes to study the class measurements and their own record sheets.

Fidel and Ryan were comparing 4 centimeters and 12 centimeters when Kathy visited their table. "How does the circumference and the diameter compare?" Kathy asked.

"It's bigger," Fidel responded. "The circumference is bigger."

"How much bigger?" Kathy queried.

Fidel looked at the numbers and then responded, "Eight centimeters."

Kathy realized that Fidel had figured the difference between the measurements rather than thinking about how many times bigger one was than the other. "How many *times* bigger is the circumference than the diameter?" She pressed.

Using one number to identify the quantity in one group (e.g., 12 cm) while the other number is the comparison factor (e.g., 4 cm) isn't an easy type of multiplication problem for students to think about. The relational language in multiplicative compare problems (e.g., *times as many as*, *times greater*) is difficult for students, especially for English language learners. Students make sense of both the language and the relationships the language implies through discussing and modeling these problems (Chapin and Johnson 2006). Having the string lengths was essential to helping students in the class when comparing the measurements.

After a few seconds, Kathy repeated her question to Fidel.

"Four times," Fidel said, hesitantly.

"Let's test it out," Kathy suggested. "Four centimeters times four is . . . ,"

"Sixteen," Fidel quickly answered. "Oh, I mean it's three times bigger. The circumference is three times bigger because four times three is twelve."

"Look at the other measurements and see if the circumference is always three times bigger," Kathy directed before she made her way back to the front of the room. When she regained students' attention, Kathy had the class compare a few more measurements. Each time, the students noticed that the circumference was about three times bigger than the diameter.

Presenting Some Hidden Circles

"It seems like you are getting pretty good at comparing the diameters and the circumferences of these circles," Kathy said. "Now I'm going to test you to see if you can *predict* what the circumference is if you only know the diameter. Who can remind us what the word *predict* means?"

"It's like a guess," Kiarra said.

"That's right," Kathy answered. "If you know the *relationship* between the circumference and the diameter of a circle, you should be able to make some good predictions, or guesses." Kathy purposefully used the word *relationship* to model mathematical language for the students. While the lesson doesn't necessarily call for students to produce the word, it is important for them to understand the word in the context of comparing a circle's measurements.

Next, Kathy told the students that she had a circle hidden behind her back. She revealed the circle's diameter: 8 centimeters. Then she told the students to talk at their tables and predict what the circumference of the hidden circle was.

The room erupted in conversation. The students were excited about predicting the circumference; it was like a guessing game to them. After about thirty seconds, Kathy called them back to attention.

"Raise your hand if you think you know what the circumference of my hidden circle is if the diameter is eight centimeters," Kathy directed the class. Nearly everyone's hand was raised. On the count of three, Kathy had everyone whisper the answer.

"Twenty-four centimeters!"

"How did you know?" Kathy asked, feigning surprise.

Using the sentence frames for support, Jorge explained, "It's because the diameter is about three times smaller than the circumference, so it's like three times eight."

Kathy revealed the hidden circle and quickly measured the circumference with string and a ruler to check everyone's prediction. Then she told the students that she had another hidden circle behind the overhead projector whose circumference measured 27 centimeters. Once again, Kathy had the students talk at their tables and predict what the circle's diameter measured.

Kathy clapped twice to regain students' attention and then waited until many hands were wiggling in the air. Manuel was especially eager to share his thinking.

"It's nine!" Manuel exclaimed, smiling from ear to ear.

"Nine what?" Kathy asked, always pushing for more language from students.

"The diameter is nine centimeters," he responded.

"Thumbs up if you agree," Kathy said to the class. It definitely looked like there was a consensus about the diameter measurement. Kathy then revealed the hidden circle and measured the diameter to check the students' prediction. The circle's diameter measured about 9 centimeters.

Writing About Diameter and Circumference

After revealing the second hidden circle, Kathy directed the students to write about what they noticed about the relationship between the diameter and the circumference of each circle. She reminded them to look at the measurements on their *Round Things* record sheet as well as the strings on their construction paper. She also encouraged them to use the sentence frames for support.

Angelita, a native English speaker, did not use the sentence frames but wrote freely, using correct syntax and grammar. Her writing indicated strong mathematical understanding. (See Figure 7–2.)

Round Things

Object	Diameter	Circumference
1. Plastic Cup	3 in.	$9\frac{1}{8}$ in
2. Diet Pepsi Can	$2\frac{3}{4}$ in.	$8\frac{1}{8}$ in
3. Chow Mein Noodle Can	4 in.	$12\frac{1}{4}$ in.
4.		
5.		

What do you notice about the relationship between the diameter and the circumference of the circles?

The relationship between the diameter and the circumference is that the Diameter is always 3 of the Circumference. If you multiply the diameter times 3 it almost equals the measurement of the Circumference. This is always the relationship.

FIGURE 7-2. Angelita's writing was very clear.

Manuel, an intermediate English language learner, successfully used the intermediate-level sentence frames to write about his thinking. While his writing indicates that he needed work with articles (*the*) and comparatives (*than*), his math thinking was correct. (See Figure 7–3.) Kathy is careful not to allow linguistic mistakes such as incorrect grammar to inhibit the recognition of good mathematical thinking.

May used the advanced frames to express her understanding. (See Figure 7–4.)

Arie was able to compare the circumference and the diameter, but she didn't go beyond a surface-level comparison. Using the sentence frames would have been beneficial, since her writing has significant syntactical errors. (See Figure 7–5.)

<table>
<tr><th colspan="3">Round Things</th></tr>
<tr><th>Object</th><th>Diameter</th><th>Circumference</th></tr>
<tr><td>1. Cup</td><td>8 cm</td><td>24 ch</td></tr>
<tr><td>2. drom</td><td>$11\frac{1}{4}$ cm</td><td>$34\frac{1}{2}$ cm</td></tr>
<tr><td>3. Spray</td><td>9 cm</td><td>23 ch</td></tr>
<tr><td>4. Peny</td><td>$6\frac{1}{2}$ cm</td><td>$1\frac{1}{4}$ cm</td></tr>
<tr><td>5.</td><td></td><td></td></tr>
</table>

What do you notice about the relationship between the diameter and the circumference of the circles?

The Diameter is 3 times smaller then circumference. the circumference is bigger than Diameter.

FIGURE 7-3. Manuel used intermediate sentence frames to explain his thinking.

Round Things

Object	Diameter	Circumference
candle 1.	2 in	6½ in
tomatoe can 2.	2½ in	8½ in
Plastic cup 3.	4½	11½
Magnet (I m in charge here) 4.	4½ in	10½ in
Penny 5.	1 in	2½ in

What do you notice about the relationship between the diameter and the circumference of the circles?

The circumference is longer than the diameter and the diameter is shorter than the circumference. The circumference is about 3 times greater than the diameter and the diameter is about 3 times smaller than the circumference.

Summarizing the Lesson

To summarize the measurement lesson, Kathy had students share their writing with a partner at their table and then had volunteers share with the whole group. When they were finished, Kathy addressed the class.

"It seems that everyone noticed that the circumference of a circle is always going to be a little more than three times the length of its diameter, and the diameter is always going to be about three times shorter than the circumference," Kathy summed up. "This is true for any circle."

Round Things

Object	Diameter	Circumference
1. Can of soup	$2\frac{1}{2}$ inch	8 inch.
2. Spray	2 inch	7 inch.
3. tenis ball	3 inch	$9\frac{1}{2}$ inch
4. olives can	$3\frac{1}{2}$ inch	$9\frac{1}{2}$ inch
5.		

What do you notice about the relationship between the diameter and the circumference of the circles?

We notice about the relationship on all the things we did are the diameter was smaller than the circumfrence because the circumfrence are bigger than the diameter.

FIGURE 7-5. Arie's writing had some syntactical errors.

Kathy then recorded this on the board:

$C \approx 3 \times D$

"This means that the circumference is about equal to three times the diameter," Kathy explained. She then wrote this on the board:

$D \approx \frac{1}{3}C$

"Who can tell us what this means?" Kathy asked.

"Does that mean that the diameter is about one-third as big as the circumference?" Daisy asked.

"Exactly," Kathy responded.

Kathy continued her explanation with a light touch. "The circumference of a circle is always going to be a little more than three times longer than its diameter," she explained. "That number that is a little more than three is a special number with its own name. It's called *pi*."

To finish the lesson, Kathy wrote *pi* on the board, along with the symbol used for it (π) and explained, "When you divide the length of the circumference of any circle by the length of the circle's diameter, the result is always pi. It will always be about three and fourteen-hundredths."

$pi \approx 3.14$

Activity
Directions ◆ **Round Things**

Day 1

Minilesson Introducing Academic Language

1. Tap students' prior knowledge by asking partners to talk about times when they have compared two things.

2. Draw two line segments on the board and label them A and B, making sure that Line A is about twice as long as Line B. Ask students to compare the two line segments.

3. Draw two new line segments on the board and label them C and D. Make Line C about four times as long as Line D. Ask the students to compare the line segments.

4. Tape a sheet of chart paper to the board and begin recording vocabulary terms that the students have used in their comparisons, such as *longer, shorter, bigger, smaller,* $\frac{1}{2}$, $\frac{1}{3}$, and $\frac{1}{4}$. Also record the beginning and intermediate sentence frames, as appropriate, with different-colored markers.

Beginning

_____ *is* _____. _____ *is* _____.

Intermediate

_____ is _____ than _____.			

_____ is _____ times _____ than _____.

_____ is _____ of _____.

Ask students to use the sentence frames to compare the line segments.

5. Next, on the board, write *5* and *25*. Have students compare these numbers using the sentence frames. Continue to add new vocabulary words, such as *multiplication, multiply, division,* and *divide,* to the vocabulary chart as they come up. Repeat the process with the numbers $20\frac{1}{2}$ and *45*. Use this as an opportunity to talk about approximation and introduce the advanced sentence frames:

_____ is about/around/approximately _____ of _____.

_____ is about/around/approximately _____ times _____ than _____.

Introducing the Lesson

1. Draw a circle on the vocabulary chart and ask the students what they know about circles. As students share with the class, reinforce the following ideas and vocabulary, and record the names of the parts of the circle on the chart next to the circle.

✦ circumference
✦ radius
✦ diameter

Have students talk about these concepts in small groups to deepen their understanding.

2. Show the class a circular object, such as a soda can, and a piece of string. Ask a volunteer to model how to measure the object's circumference and diameter with the piece of string and a ruler. Using an

enlarged version of the *Round Things* record sheet, show the students how to record their data. Then show them how to tape their strings to a piece of construction paper and label them.

3. Distribute the materials to partners and let them get to work. Each pair should find the diameters and circumferences of five circular objects. For each circular object, partners should do the following:

    a. Take a piece of string and wrap it around the circumference, cut the string, and then measure the string to find the circumference measurement. Then place a string across the circle's diameter, cut the string, and measure the string to find the diameter measurement.

    b. Tape the two strings that measure the circle's circumference and diameter onto a piece of construction paper in order to compare their lengths (do this for each circular object, for a total of five pairs of strings on the construction paper). Label the circumference *C* and the diameter *D* and label each pair of strings with the object's name.

    c. Record the name of the object, the diameter measurement, and the circumference measurement on the *Round Things* record sheet.

Day 2

A Class Discussion

1. Give students time to complete the measuring. When partners have finished measuring and recording their circular objects, ask them to look at their data and tell what they notice. Then take a piece of string that represents the circumference of a circle and a piece of string that represents the diameter of the circle and place them on the overhead. Ask students to compare the string lengths using the sentence frames.

2. Have partners compare the lengths of each of their circles' diameter and circumference using the sentence frames for support. Have partners share what they observed with the class.

3. Elicit numerical measurements of several partners' circular objects, recording the diameters and circumferences on a class chart. Ask students to look at the numbers and see if they can make statements about the relationship between the circumferences and diameters using the sentence frames.

4. Ask the students if they can predict what the circumference of a circle will be based on its diameter. Encourage students to use frames to note the relationships they discovered as a basis for making a prediction. Use verbal prompts such as "I predict" and "I think" to help students express their ideas.

5. Tell students that you have a circle hidden from view. Tell them what the diameter of the circle is. Ask them to talk with a partner and make a prediction about what they think the circle's circumference measures and why. Have students share their thinking with the class. Reveal the circle and tell what the circumference measures.

6. Tell the students that you have another circle hidden from view. This time, tell the students what the circumference measures. Ask them to discuss with a partner what they think the diameter of the circle measures and why. Have students share their thinking, and then reveal the circle's diameter.

7. Have students write a summary about the relationship between the circumferences and diameters of the circles at the bottom of their *Round Things* record sheet, using the sentence frames if needed.

8. Ask students to share their writing with a partner, then have a few volunteers read their writing to the class. With a light touch, hold a class discussion on the concept of pi. Explain that the relationship between the diameter and the circumference of any circle is always the same no matter the size of the circle. When the circumference of a circle is divided by its diameter, the result will always be approximately 3.14, and this number is known as pi.

Round Things

8 Helping English Language Learners Make Sense of Math Word Problems

English language learners (ELLs) typically experience difficulty under-standing and therefore solving math word problems for a variety of reasons. Word problems require slower and more careful reading than other prose because of the technical words and symbols and the complex concepts that they contain (Carrasquilo and Segan 1998). Consider the following problem from a fifth-grade math textbook:

> The greatest amount of honey Mrs. Canseco's bees ever made in one week was $6\frac{3}{4}$ pounds. The least amount of honey her bees ever made in one week was $2\frac{1}{4}$ pounds. What is the difference between the greatest and least amount of honey the bees made in a week? (McGraw-Hill, 2002)

This relatively short paragraph is packed with information that a student needs to understand in order to figure the answer. Through-out the problem, the reader confronts symbols that represent a mix of whole numbers and fractions as well as the following mathematically related words: *greatest amount, least amount, pounds, difference, between,* and *week.*

The vocabulary used in math word problems is another source of difficulty for English language learners. Understanding vocabulary is crucial; almost every word, number, and symbol carries important meaning, and misunderstanding just one word in a story problem can prevent a student from being able to find a solution. English learners can become confused if the mathematical vocabulary has different meanings in everyday usage, as with *even, odd, function,* and *operation.* Words such as *sum* and *whole* can also cause confusion for English learners because they have nonmathematical homophones.

Another obstacle is a student's incomplete understanding of syn-tax and grammar. For example, word problems are often embedded in language that makes the problems unclear or difficult to comprehend. Consider the following problem from a third-grade textbook:

Tina's mom brought 3 packs of soda to the party.
Each pack had 6 sodas.
How many sodas did she bring to the party? (McGraw-Hill, 2002)

This word problem uses both the past and the present tenses of the irregular verb *to bring* in one question, which may cause difficulty for an ELL, depending on the student's English language proficiency. In addition, the use of the possessive *Tina's mom* could be confusing to English learners if possessives are not used in their native language, as in Spanish (in Spanish, *Tina's mom* would read *la mamá de Tina*, or *the mother of Tina*). Also, the word used to describe the grouping of sodas is *pack*, another multiple-meaning word that may not be common to the working vocabulary of an English language learner.

In addition to the linguistic demands presented by math word problems, English language learners must also contend with the specific details included in each problem. In theory, these details provide a context for the problem. In reality, they often serve to further obfuscate the question being posed. While the purpose for the details is to create a context that is more applicable to real-life mathematical situations than straight computation, the inadvertent result is a context that may be completely unrelated to the lives of ELLs. The following problem illustrates how the context of a math word problem can carry a cultural bias:

The Scouts clean the trailhead parking lot each spring. There are 28 Scouts who have signed up for the cleanup. If the Scouts are evenly divided among 7 groups, how many are in each group? (McGraw-Hill, 2002)

The details in this problem make sense to someone who participates in children's service organizations and spends time hiking. While these details are often cumbersome even for native English speakers, English language learners may find them foreign and intimidating.

Solving math word problems requires mathematical insight and knowledge *as well as* a sensitivity to language. Therefore, it is important to realize that in addition to math skills, ELLs must also possess the reading skills necessary to solve math word problems. When posing word problems to English language learners, a focus on reading *and* math skills is essential.

Whatever language or math skills English language learners possess, it is important that they have opportunities to make sense of the mathematics in their own way once the barrier of language is lifted. For example, a teacher in a fourth-grade classroom posed the following math word problem for students to solve:

I want to find the total number of pennies in 7 rolls of pennies.
I know each roll has 50 pennies.

The teacher first read the problem aloud with the students. She then showed the class seven rolls of pennies. Several students, all English language learners, were surprised when they saw the money rolls. They commented that when they initially read the problem, they thought *rolls* meant *candy*. The teacher then used the penny rolls to help the class understand what fifty pennies *in each* roll meant. Using realia (objects from the environment) helped the students clarify the language in the problem. Once the barrier of language was removed, the teacher allowed each student to solve the problem in a way that made sense to her or him. For example, José drew pictures of penny rolls and skip-counted by fifties to find the answer (see Figure 8–1). Angélica looked at the number patterns in equations, starting with the basic fact of 7 × 5 (see Figure 8–2).

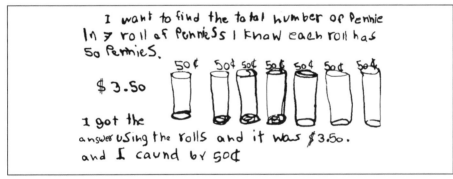

FIGURE 8-1.
José skip-counted to arrive at the correct answer.

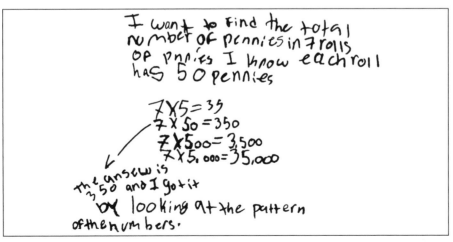

FIGURE 8-2.
Angélica used multiplication to solve the problem.

Strategies That Help English Learners Make Sense of Math Word Problems

Following is a list of teaching strategies that can help all students, especially English language learners, make sense of and solve math word problems. Determining which strategy to use depends upon the word problem being posed (also see Chapter 9 for examples of these strategies being used in a math lesson).

- Have students practice reading the problem aloud together, and then ask the following questions:
  - What do you know?
  - Is anything confusing (words, phrases)?
  - What do you have to find out?
  - What numbers and operations will you use to solve the problem?
- Use synonyms for unfamiliar words (e.g., names of people and places).
- Identify multiple-meaning words and homophones (words that are pronounced in the same way but have different meanings and sometimes spellings) and clarify their meanings.
- Model retelling the problem using synonyms or gestures for difficult words, and then have students practice retelling the problem.
- Write two different word problems on the board and have the students compare and contrast them. Analyzing word problems can help students think about important vocabulary words that have the same meaning (e.g., *in all* and *altogether*). Scrutinizing word problems can also give students practice with identifying the important elements in the problem while learning to disregard parts that are not essential to finding a solution.
- Act out the problem or use realia (e.g., money) to model the problem.
- Draw a picture or chart to help students visualize the problem and/or have students sketch a picture of their solution strategy.
- Ask students clarifying questions, and then have them go back to the text to prove their answers.
- Help students become aware of complex or difficult syntax.
- Help students identify what the numbers stand for in the problem.

+ Have students write their own word problems, providing sentence frames and a vocabulary bank for support.
+ Pose word problems in contexts that are familiar to students.

Word Problem Examples and Possible Strategies to Use

Word Problem

Jacob had 2 quarters, 3 dimes, 2 nickels, and 1 penny.
He spent 3 of the coins at the store.
What is the least amount of money Jacob could have left? The greatest amount?

Strategies

+ Have students use real coins to model the problem.
+ Review the value of each of the coins and what each coin looks like.
+ Use synonyms for the words *greatest* (e.g., *most*) and *least* (e.g., *smallest amount*).
+ Discuss the multiple-meaning word *left* by giving examples of the different meanings of the word (e.g., After I bought my candy, I had only four cents *left*. When you get to the street, turn *left*.).

Word Problem

Ben used a coupon to pay for a purchase at the grocery store.
The original price of his purchase was $12.00.
The coupon reduced the price to $7.50.
What was the value of the coupon?

Strategies

+ Use synonyms for *coupon, purchase, original, reduced,* and *value.*
+ Draw upon your bilingual students in the class; they can help by translating difficult words and identifying words in the problem that may be cognates (e.g., *original* and *coupon* have Spanish cognates).
+ Have students retell the problem in their own words.

Word Problem

There were 12 students playing basketball.
Two-thirds of the students were boys.
How many boys were playing basketball?

Strategies

✦ Draw a picture to model the problem.
✦ Have the students act out the problem.
✦ Ask clarifying questions, and then have students go back to the text to prove their answers. Examples of clarifying questions include

  ✦ Were there only boys playing basketball? How do you know?
  ✦ How many boys and girls were playing basketball? How do you know?
  ✦ Were there more girls or boys playing? How do you know?
  ✦ Were there more or less than twelve boys playing basketball? How do you know?

✦ Have students write their own word problems and provide sentence frames for support. In addition, brainstorm with the students a list of whole numbers, fractions, and verbs that will help them write their problems.

Sample Problem

There were _____ *students* _____.
number verb

_____ *of the students were* _____.
fraction boys/girls

How many _____ *were* _____?
boys/girls verb

Sample Word Bank

Whole Numbers: six (6), ten (10), twelve (12), fifteen (15), twenty (20), twenty-five (25), thirty (30)

Fractions: one-third ($\frac{1}{3}$), one-half ($\frac{1}{2}$), two-thirds ($\frac{2}{3}$), one-fourth ($\frac{1}{4}$), three-fourths ($\frac{3}{4}$)

Verbs: reading, playing, running, studying, eating lunch

Word Problem

Mr. and Mrs. Gregorio took their five children to the fair.
Each child in the family got $4 less than the next older brother or sister to spend at the fair.
If the oldest child received $20, how much did the youngest receive?

Strategies

✦ Draw pictures to represent the problem.
✦ Clarify difficult syntax such as the second sentence of the problem.
✦ Have students retell the problem in their own words.

Word Problem

On Sunday the temperature reached a low of 15 degrees. The low fell by 2 degrees every day until Saturday, when the low temperature rose to 10 degrees. What was the mean low temperature for the week?

Strategies

✦ Make a chart (including the days of the week) to visualize and organize the problem.
✦ Clarify the meanings of the words *temperature, degrees, fell,* and *rose.*
✦ Discuss the multiple-meaning word *mean* by giving examples of the different meanings of the word (e.g., That man has a *mean* look on his face. I don't understand what you *mean* by that. What was the *mean* low temperature for the week?).

Word Problem

The neighborhood bakery sold 513 loaves of bread last month.
If it takes 3 cups of flour to make each loaf of bread, about how many cups of flour were used?

Strategies

✦ Use realia (loaf of bread, cup of flour) to help bring meaning to the problem. Focus particular attention on the word *flour* and explicitly make a distinction for students between *flower* and *flour*.

✦ Have the students retell the problem with a partner.

✦ Ask students what the word *about* means. Gesture by moving your hands up and down to show the meaning of the word. Tell the students that they will need to *estimate* to find out *about how many cups*. Talk about what *estimating* means, connecting it to the more familiar word *guess*.

Removing the Barrier of Language

Story problems are just math problems with words. But for a student who is learning a second (or third) language, words in that new language can create a barrier to understanding. By explicitly teaching English in math class and providing well-designed extra support that focuses on math and reading skills, teachers can help remove the roadblock of language that often prevents English language learners from making sense of and therefore solving math word problems. In fact, the challenges that vocabulary, grammar, and syntax pose to English learners can become English language development opportunities in math class.

Some ELLs, especially those with beginning- and intermediate-level skills, will most likely need help understanding the language used in math word problems. Once they understand the language, they should be able to successfully focus on the mathematics and solve the problem. Other English learners, especially those who also struggle with mathematics, may need support with language *and* math.

Whatever language or math skills your English learners possess, it is important that students have opportunities to make sense of the mathematics in their own way once the barrier of language is lifted.

9 Writing and Solving Multiplication and Division Word Problems

Overview

This lesson gives children experience writing and then solving multiplication and division word problems. First, the class creates a chart with a list of things that come in sets of 2s, 3s, 4s, 5s, and so on, up to 12s. The students then use the items on the lists, and sentence frames provided, to write stories. After they write stories, each student creates and then solves three different word problems based on the story that she has written. Finally, the students compare their word problems with new word problems from their math textbook and use a variety of strategies to make sense of and solve the new word problems.

Math Goal: Students will connect real-world situations to multiplication and division equations and identify and use the relationships between operations to solve problems.

Language Goal: Students will describe multiplication and division situations and summarize computational strategies.

Key Vocabulary: addition/add, altogether, division/divide, in all, multiplication/multiply, operation, subtraction/subtract, total, unknown

Materials

✦ 3 sheets of chart paper
✦ half sheets of writing paper, at least 6 per student
✦ 1 4-by-4-inch square of construction paper

Sentence Frames That Help Students Write Multiplication and Division Word Problems

All Students

> *There are* _____ _____ .

> *Each* _____ *has* _____ _____ .

> *There are* _____ _____ *altogether.*

Class Profile

In Mrs. Gómez's class of thirty students, there are six beginning-level English language learners (ELLs), six intermediate-level ELLs, and five students with advanced fluency in English. The remaining students are native English speakers.

 From the Classroom

✦ Multiplication and Division Word Problems, Day 1

Minilesson Introducing Academic Language

The day before Christine came to Mrs. Gómez's class to teach, the students had brainstormed lists of things that come in sets of 2s, 3s, 4s, 5s, and so on, up to 12s. Mrs. Gómez compiled the lists on a class chart:

Things That Come in Groups

2s	3s	4s	5s	6s	7s
pair of socks	sides on a triangle	wheels on a car	toes on one foot	sodas in one pack	days in a week
eyes on a person	wheels on a tricycle	legs on a tiger	sides on a pentagon	legs on an insect	
shoes in a pair		corners on a square		colors in a rainbow	

(Continued)

8s	9s	10s	11s	12s
legs on an octopus legs on a spider	planets in our solar system players on the field in a soccer game	fingers on two hands	players on the field in a game of football	months in a year eggs in a dozen hours on a clock

During the creation of the list, Mrs. Gómez became aware of the students' need for some vocabulary development. While they could easily name items that came in the various quantities (five fingers on a hand, eight legs on a spider, and so on), many of them could not name the less commonly used terms for groupings. For example, they knew that eggs came in groups of twelve, but they didn't immediately come up with *dozen*. They knew that shoes and socks came in twos, but they didn't all know the term *pair*. This posed a problem for the English language learners as they tried to refer to the items on the chart. They could easily say, "There are three spiders," to refer to three groups of eight legs. They could not, however, form a similar statement for shoes. They said things like, "There are three shoes," when they meant three *pairs* of shoes. It is crucial that students discuss and learn the relevant grouping terms during the creation of the list so that they can use them easily later in the lesson. (A children's book that explains and illustrates grouping terms like these is *More Than One*, by Miriam Schlein [1996].)

When Christine came to teach her lesson, she began by asking the students to remind her of the things on the lists.

"What comes in twos?" she asked the class.

"Eyes!"

"Ears!"

"What about threes?" Christine continued.

"Triangles!" Tam exclaimed.

"Do triangles come in threes, or is there something *on* a triangle that comes in threes?" Christine asked, trying to help Tam clarify.

Tam thought for a moment but looked a little confused. To help, Christine quickly sketched a triangle on the board, making the idea visible. Tam responded, "Oh, three sides! Each triangle has three sides."

Christine continued asking students to name at least one item from each of the lists on the chart. She then pointed to the sentence frames she had written on another chart and told the students that they would be using the frames to help them write stories:

| There are _____ _____. |

| Each _____ has _____ _____. |

| There are _____ _____ altogether. |

"You're going to fill in what's missing in the blank spaces and turn the sentence frames into a story," Christine told the class. "Who would like to suggest a number from two to twelve?"

"How about eight," Moses said.

Christine pointed to the space on the "Things That Come in Groups" chart that had suggestions for sets of eight. She chose *legs on a spider.*

"Now we have to think about how many spiders we want in our story," she said to the class. "How about three spiders." On the board, below the chart on which the sentence frames were written, Christine wrote the first sentence in the story. She underlined the number and word that filled the blank spaces in the sentence frames so the students could see how she completed the frame:

| There are <u>3</u> <u>spiders</u>. |

"How many legs does each spider have?" Christine asked.

"Eight!" the students chorused. Christine wrote the second sentence in the story, using the sentence frames and underlining the words and number that filled the blank spaces:

| Each <u>spider</u> has <u>8</u> <u>legs</u>. |

"And what do you think my third sentence will say? What's going to go in the blank spaces?" Christine asked. She gave the class a few seconds of think time and then called on Vic. Vic is an English language learner with advanced fluency; he has also been identified by the school district as a gifted student.

"Your last sentence will say that there are twenty-four legs altogether," Vic said.

"How did you know that?" Christine asked, pushing for an explanation.

"I multiplied," Vic responded.

"What did you multiply?" Christine probed.

"Three times eight," he explained. "It's three spiders times eight legs each, and that's twenty-four legs altogether."

Christine wrote the third sentence in the story, again underlining the word and number that filled the blank spaces:

There are 24 legs altogether.

"So there are twenty-four legs altogether," Christine said. "*Altogether* means that we're counting all the legs on each of the three spiders. Let's see if Vic is correct."

Christine then quickly sketched three spiders on the board, each with eight legs. Along with the students, she counted the legs, one by one, to check whether there were indeed twenty-four.

"Vic was correct; there are twenty-four legs altogether," she said. "Vic multiplied three spiders times eight legs, which is much faster than counting by ones, like we did."

Christine then had the students read aloud the story that she had written:

There are 3 spiders.
Each spider has 8 legs.
There are 24 legs altogether.

After the students practiced reading the story, Christine wrote these directions for writing a story on the board:

1. *Choose a number from the chart.*
2. *Choose an item from the list.*
3. *Think of how many of the item will be in your story.*
4. *Write a story using the sentence frames.*
5. *Draw a picture of your story.*

Christine told the students to think of a number and an item from the list, then turn and tell a partner. She then checked in with the students, asking each what number and item he or she had chosen for his or her story. When she was sure that everyone had an idea for a story, she handed out a half sheet of paper to each student and the class got to work.

Writing Math Stories

Most students wrote their stories with little difficulty, assisted by the sentence frames and the "Things That Come in Groups" chart. Some students, however, had trouble thinking about what the group was in their story and what they were trying to find the total for.

Pablo, a beginning-level English speaker who is a recent arrival in the country, chose shoes for his item from the list of things that come in sets of two. He began his story by writing:

There are 2 shoes.
Each shoes

When Christine visited his table, he was stuck and didn't know how to move forward with his story. Addressing all four students at the table, Christine asked, "Does anyone know what we call it when there are two shoes together?"

"Pair," Vic responded. "It's called a pair of shoes."

"Yeah, it's not like the *pear* that you eat," Naomi chimed in, referring to the homophones *pair* and *pear*.

Using English experts as resources is a helpful strategy. Over time, beginning-level English speakers like Pablo can learn to ask other students for help with English instead of always relying on the teacher.

To assist him, Christine asked Pablo the following questions:

✦ How many pairs of shoes are there in your story?
✦ How many shoes are in each pair?
✦ How many shoes are there altogether?

Before Pablo finished his story, Christine had him draw a picture of two pairs of shoes. This helped him bring meaning to his story and figure the total number of shoes. (See Figure 9–1.)

Valerie had trouble with her story as well. She chose planets in the solar system from the list of things that come in sets of nine. In her first

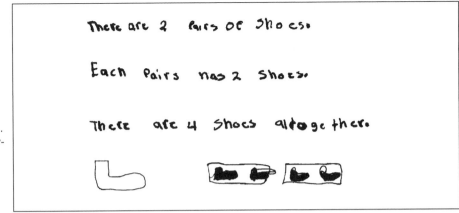

FIGURE 9–1. Pablo's drawing helped him understand the story problem.

There are 2 pairs of shoes.

Each pairs has 2 shoes.

There are 4 shoes altogether.

draft, she wrote:

There are ~~9~~ 8 planets.
Each planet has 9 solar systems.
There are _____ _____ altogether.

Valerie knew what a planet was but was not familiar with the term *solar system* and did not understand that the solar system, in this case, was the *group*, and the planets were the things *in the group*. As with Pablo, Christine modeled getting help from some English experts at Valerie's table.

"Who knows what a solar system is?" Christine asked.

"It's like our solar system, with the planets," Roxana said.

"There are nine planets in the solar system," Josh added.

Loren, whose native language is the same as Valerie's, used Spanish as a resource and explained, "Solar system is almost the same in Spanish. It's *el sistema solar*. Los planetas en el sistema solar [The planets in the solar system]."

"So a solar system in your story is a *group* of planets," Christine told Valerie. "And there are nine planets in each group, or solar system." Christine then asked Valerie the following questions:

✦ How many solar systems are in your story?
✦ How many planets are in each solar system?
✦ How many planets are there altogether?

As with Pablo, Christine directed Valerie to draw a picture *before* writing her story. (See Figure 9–2.)

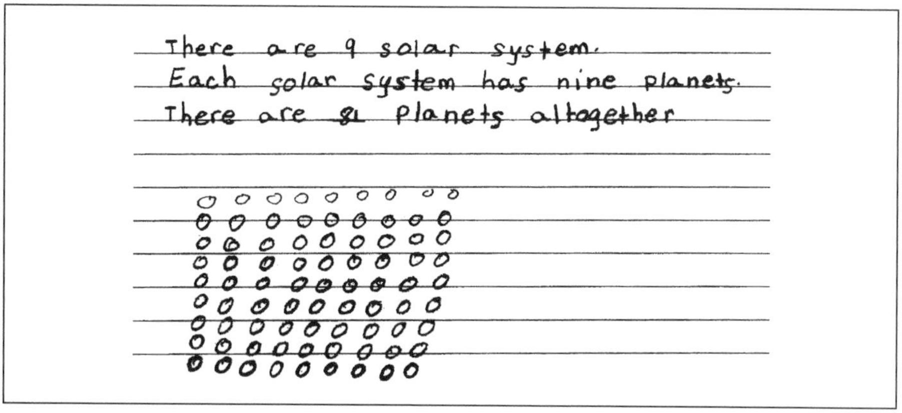

There are 9 solar system.
Each solar system has nine planets.
There are 81 planets altogether

FIGURE 9-2.
Valerie drew
a picture to
help her
write the
story.

When the students were finished writing, Christine had partners read their stories to one another, and then she asked for volunteers to share their stories with the class.

Writing the stories helped students think about the notion of equal groups, an important idea in multiplication and division situations. Writing stories also familiarized students with the language they would need in order to write their own math word problems.

Writing Word Problems

To begin the second part of the lesson, Christine wrote the word *unknown* on the chart next to the sentence frames and had the students read it aloud. She then asked them if they knew the meaning of the word.

"Is it someone that you don't know?" Amandita guessed.

"It means no one knows you," Chris added.

"That would be an unknown person," Christine said. "But what if I'm talking about an unknown number?"

"It means a *number* that you don't know," Tam responded.

"Exactly," Christine acknowledged. She then wrote this equation on the board:

$$6 \times \underline{\hspace{1cm}} = 18$$

"Where is the *unknown?*" Christine asked the class.

"In the middle!" students answered.

"That's right," Christine responded. "An *unknown* number is like a mystery; we don't yet know what it is. What would the unknown

Writing and Solving Multiplication and Division Word Problems   *145*

number be in this problem?" Christine asked as she wrote the following equation on the board:

$$\underline{\hspace{1.5cm}} \times 3 = 18$$

"Six!" students chorused.

"What is the unknown number in this problem?" Christine asked as she wrote another equation on the board:

$$6 \times 3 = \underline{\hspace{1.5cm}}$$

"Eighteen!" the students responded with ease.

To model how to use the students' stories to write math word problems, Christine began by pointing to the story she had originally written about spiders:

There are 3 spiders.
Each spider has 8 legs.
There are 24 legs altogether.

"I'm going to turn this story about spiders into a math word problem," Christine told the class. "First, I'm going to start at the bottom with the third sentence, and cover up the number in the sentence." Christine took a 4-by-4-inch piece of construction paper and taped it to the board to cover the number 24:

There are 3 spiders.
Each spider has 8 legs.
There are ▇ legs altogether.

"Do you see where the *unknown* is?" Christine asked the class, emphasizing the new word students had just learned. "What is the unknown in this problem?"

"Twenty-four!" Amandita exclaimed.

"Yes," Christine acknowledged, "twenty-four is the unknown number that we're looking for, but what is the unknown information in the problem? What are we trying to find out?"

"We're trying to figure out how many legs there are on all the spiders," Chris responded.

"Yes, that's correct," Christine said. "To turn this story into a math problem, we have to make the last sentence a question. Turn to a partner and talk about how we can turn the last sentence into a question that we have to answer."

As partners shared their ideas, Christine quickly made a lap around the room, listening in on students' conversations. After about thirty seconds, she asked for the students' attention. "Can we ask, 'How many spiders altogether?'" Christine asked.

"No!" several students exclaimed.

"Look, you already know how many spiders—there are three," Moses chimed in matter-of-factly.

"So what question can we ask?" Christine queried.

"How many legs are there altogether?" Naomi suggested. There were nods of agreement all around. Christine rewrote the story, creating the first math problem, and then directed the students to read it aloud.

Math Problem 1

There are 3 spiders.
Each spider has 8 legs.
How many legs are there altogether?

Pointing to her original story about spiders, Christine thought out loud, "What other numbers can I make unknown?" She waited a few seconds so that the students could ponder this question as well. Then she took the construction paper square off the number 24 and placed it over the 8 in the second sentence of the story:

There are 3 spiders.
Each spider has ▮ legs.
There are 24 legs altogether.

"Now eight is the unknown number in our story," Christine told the class. "So in the second problem we're going to write, the unknown is the number of legs on . . . ," she prompted.

"On each spider!" the students responded.

"Let's write the second math word problem," Christine said. "What do I start with? Are there any sentences we can leave the same?"

Following students' suggestions, Christine wrote the first two sentences in the word problem:

There are 3 spiders.
There are 24 legs altogether.

Writing and Solving Multiplication and Division Word Problems

"Now turn to a partner and talk about what the question is going to be for our third sentence in the math word problem," Christine directed. As before, she made a quick lap around the room. As Christine circulated, listening in on students' conversations, she realized how difficult the irregular verb *does* is for English language learners. Many of the students in the class didn't think of using the word, and several were using it incorrectly, such as "How many legs do each spider have?" Some students correctly crafted a question without using the word *does*. For example, Christine heard one boy say, "How many legs are there on each spider?" Other students used the word *altogether* when it wasn't necessary, saying, "How many legs does each spider have altogether?"

Listening to the students helped inform Christine's next teaching move. She knew that she needed to focus students' attention on understanding the language used in creating word problems, thereby giving them the skills to interpret and solve math word problems. This focus on language in math class benefits all students, but it is crucial for English learners.

When she regained the students' attention, Christine asked, "For the question in our math word problem, do I need to use the word *altogether*?" She waited a few seconds and then called on Loren.

"No, 'cause we just want to ask how many legs on each spider," Loren explained. "We already know how many legs altogether."

"What will the first words be in our question?" Christine asked the class. "What were the first two words we used in our first math problem that we wrote?"

"How many!" the students chorused.

"How many . . . ," Christine prompted.

"How many legs on each spider?" Vic chimed in.

"How many legs does . . . ," Christine prompted further, writing the word *does* on the board near the word *unknown* so that it would be more available to the students.

"How many legs does each spider have?" Jen guessed.

"That's right," Christine confirmed. She then completed the second math word problem and had the students read it aloud:

Math Problem 2

There are 3 spiders.
There are 24 legs altogether.
How many legs does each spider have?

To help students begin to think about writing the third math word problem, Christine covered up the last unknown in her original story about spiders:

There are ▪ spiders.
Each spider has 8 legs.
There are 24 legs altogether.

At this point, the students were catching on, and with Christine's help they were able to write the third math word problem.

Math Problem 3

There are 24 legs altogether.
Each spider has 8 legs.
How many spiders are there?

When they were finished, the class had used the original spider story to write three different word problems: a multiplication situation (Math Problem 1) and two division situations (Math Problems 2 and 3). In Problem 2, the number of groups (spiders) is known, but the number of legs in each group is unknown. In Problem 3, the number of groups (spiders) is unknown while the number of legs in each group is known.

Christine gave students directions for writing the math word problems:

1. Write three problems, each on a different half sheet of paper.
2. Each math problem has to have the unknown in a different place.
3. Each problem has to end in a question.

After giving the directions, Christine distributed three half sheets of paper to each student and then the class got to work.

The students wrote with enthusiasm, working independently for the most part, and getting assistance from each other when needed. (See Figures 9–3, 9–4, and 9–5.) Christine mostly helped students figure out which sentence in their story would serve as the question to be answered.

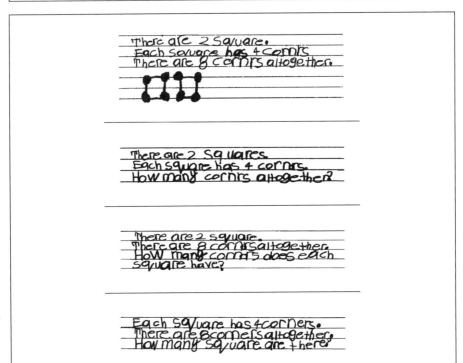

There are 5 bugs.
Each bug has six legs.
There are 30 legs, in altogether.

There are 5 bugs.
Each bug has six legs.
How many legs are there altogether?

There are 5 bugs.
There are 30 legs altogether.
How many legs does each bug have?

6

bugs

Each bug has six legs.
There are 30 legs altogether.
How many bugs are there?

FIGURE 9-3.
Jared wrote
riddles about
bugs.

There are 2 square.
Each square has 4 cornrs
There are 8 cornrs altogether.

There are 2 squares.
Each square has 4 cornrs.
How many cornrs altogether?

There are 2 square.
There are 8 cornrs altogether.
How many cornrs does each
square have?

Each square has 4 corners.
There are 8 corners altogether.
How many square are there?

FIGURE 9-4.
Abby wrote
riddles that
integrated
geometry.

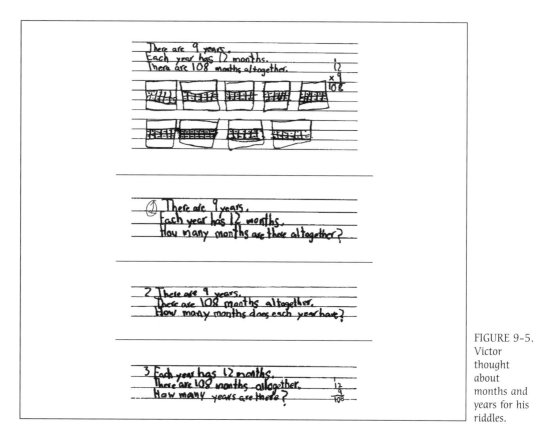

There are 9 years.
Each year has 12 months.
There are 108 months altogether.

      12
    × 9
     108

① There are 9 years.
Each year has 12 months.
How many months are there altogether?

② There are 9 years.
There are 108 months altogether.
How many months does each year have?

③ Each year has 12 months.
There are 108 months altogether.
How many years are there?

      12
    × 9
     108

FIGURE 9-5.
Victor
thought
about
months and
years for his
riddles.

✦ Multiplication and Division Word Problems, Day 2

Solving the Word Problems

The students spent about fifteen minutes at the beginning of math time putting the finishing touches on their math word problems. As students were working, Christine asked Josh if she could use one of his problems as an example. After getting his permission, she wrote the problem on the board:

> *Each bug has 6 legs.*
> *There are 30 legs altogether.*
> *How many bugs are there?*

When students were finished writing, Christine called for their attention and directed them to read aloud Josh's problem. Afterward, Christine addressed the group. "When you are solving a word problem, the first thing that you can do to help you solve it is to think about what you already know. Talk at your tables about what you know about Josh's problem. Remember, I don't want you to solve the problem yet, just talk about what you know."

After about thirty seconds, Christine regained their attention and called on Abby.

"We know that each bug has six legs," she said.

"And there are thirty legs altogether," Enrique added.

"What is the *unknown* information in the problem?" Christine asked, pointing to the word *unknown* on the class chart and writing a question mark next to the word to provide a symbol for its meaning.

"We have to find out how many bugs there are," Loren responded with confidence.

"That's right," Christine said. "To figure how many bugs there are, I want you to think about what numbers you'll have to use and what operation you'll use. Does anyone know what the word *operation* means?"

As she spoke to the class, Christine wrote the word *operation* on the class chart. Because the word has mathematical and nonmathematical meanings, Christine wanted to make sure that students understood what she meant (see the Appendix for a list of multiple-meaning words in mathematics).

"It's when a doctor operates on you," Loren said.

"In math, it means like what you do to solve a math problem," Chris posited.

"Well, you're both correct," Christine told them. "But today, we're not going to cut anyone open and operate on them, so we'll use *operation* as it relates to math." The students laughed.

Christine wrote + underneath the word *operation* on the chart and told the students that addition is an operation in mathematics. She also wrote − next to the word and said that subtraction is also an operation.

"Can anyone think of any other operations?"

"Multiplication!" several students called out.

"And division!" Vic exclaimed.

Christine recorded the symbols for multiplication and division (× and ÷) next to the word *operation*; she also wrote the words *multiplication/multiply, division/divide, addition/add,* and *subtraction/subtract* on the vocabulary chart. Christine then distributed a stack of half sheets of paper to each table and gave the students about a minute to work on Josh's word problem. When the time was up, Christine called for students' attention. "Who would like to tell us your answer and explain your thinking?" she asked.

"I did six times five is thirty," Victoria reported. Victoria is an intermediate-level English language learner. "I did six times what number makes thirty." Although Josh's problem is a division situation, Victoria was able to solve the problem using multiplication. Identifying and using the relationships between operations to solve problems is an important skill.

"What operation did you use to solve Josh's problem?" Christine asked.

"Multiplication," Victoria responded. "It's like times."

As Victoria dictated, Christine recorded on the board the equation that she used:

$$6 \times 5 = 30$$

To help students think about what the numbers in the equation represented, Christine asked, "Which number stands for the bugs?"

"The five, that's the number that we have to figure out," Pedro said.

"So five is the unknown," Christine clarified, placing a little square of construction paper over the number 5 in the equation:

$$6 \times \blacksquare = 30$$

"What does the six stand for?" Christine asked the class.

"It's the legs," Jen answered.

"The legs on each bug, or the legs altogether?" Christine probed.

"On each bug!" students exclaimed.

Christine continued with the same line of questioning, helping students match the numbers with the different parts of the word problem. "What does the thirty stand for in the equation or number sentence?" she asked. Christine waited to give the class some think time, then called on Chris.

"The thirty means the legs altogether," he replied.

On the board, Christine wrote the word that each number stood for in the problem:

$$\begin{array}{ccc} 6 & \times & 5 & = 30 \\ \text{legs} & & \text{bugs} & \text{legs altogether} \end{array}$$

Knowing that students would encounter problems with different wording and phrasing, Christine probed for synonyms. "What are some other words that mean the same as *altogether*?" "Total," one student called out.

"In all," was another response. Christine wrote these words next to the word *altogether* on the vocabulary chart.

"Did anyone use a different operation to solve the problem?" Christine inquired.

"I did thirty legs divided by six legs each and got the answer five," Roxie explained. There were nods of agreement from many of the students.

On the board, Christine wrote:

$30 \div 6 = 5$

Next, Christine asked Loren if she could share her word problem with the class, and then she wrote the problem on the board:

There are 3 poison ivy plants.
Each plant has 3 leaves.
How many leaves are there altogether?

As with Josh's story about bugs, Christine had the students think about the following questions after reading the problem aloud:

◆ What do you know?
◆ What do you need to find out?
◆ What numbers and operation(s) will you use to solve the problem?

After a brief discussion, the students got to work solving the problem. To figure the answer, most students used multiplication ($3 \times 3 = 9$) and some used repeated addition ($3 + 3 + 3 = 9$). When they were finished, Christine had a few students share their solution strategies. Once again, she helped them think about where the unknown was in the problem and what the numbers stood for. After the class discussion, Christine gave the students about five minutes to solve one another's problems.

Making Sense of Word Problems

While students were busy at work, Christine wrote a problem from their textbook (McGraw-Hill, 2002) alongside Loren's problem about poison ivy; she wanted to give students an opportunity to compare and contrast the problems.

> *There are 3 poison ivy plants.*
> *Each plant has 3 leaves.*
> *How many leaves are there altogether?*

> *A fourth grade student named Daniel puts 9 books on each of 8 shelves. How many books does he have in all?*

After the students read the new problem aloud, Christine directed them to talk in their groups about how the problems were alike and how they were different. After about a minute, Christine asked the students to report what they had discussed. Following are their comments, which Christine recorded on chart paper.

How Are the Two Problems the Same?

✦ You can solve both problems using the same operation: multiplication.
✦ You can use addition to solve both problems.
✦ You have to solve both problems.
✦ The question is the same: you have to find out how much of something altogether.
✦ *In all* and *altogether* mean the same thing.
✦ They are both stories.
✦ They both have an unknown.

How Are the Two Problems Different?

✦ They have different numbers.
✦ Different things in them: one has plants, the other has books and shelves.
✦ One problem is longer.

Having the students compare the word problems helped them focus on what they already knew and what they had to find out. It also helped them see that although one problem may be longer or worded differently than another, they can both be solved in the same way.

After comparing the two problems, Christine shifted the students' attention to solving the new problem. "Drawing a picture of the word problem can help you understand it," she pointed out. Although Christine was aware that most students in the class knew what books and bookshelves were, she had them all point to the bookshelf in the class and count the number of shelves. This was particularly helpful for the beginning English learners like Pablo, Abby, and Eva.

Christine continued, "If you were going to draw a picture of the problem, how many shelves would your drawing have?"

"Nine shelves!" several students called out.

"Are you sure?" Christine countered. "Read the problem again."

Going back to the text helped the students, and they soon realized that there would need to be eight shelves, with nine books on each shelf. To bring meaning to problems, teachers often ask students to draw pictures, but they don't always provide the support for *how* to draw them. Asking key questions (e.g., How many shelves would your drawing have?) can help students, especially ELLs, focus on and then visualize the elements in the word problem: the number of groups (shelves) and the number in each group (books).

Christine then gave the students a few minutes to solve the problem, directing them to provide an equation and a drawing. (See Figure 9–6.)

When the students had finished working, Christine pulled them back together and had a few volunteers share their solution strategies. Then she wrote a final problem on the board; this one was also from the students' textbook:

Mrs. Palmer has a collection of 54 Ukrainian eggs.
She gives each of her 6 grandchildren the same number of eggs.
How many eggs does Mrs. Palmer give each grandchild? (McGraw-Hill, 2002)

After reading the problem aloud with the class, Christine asked the students to discuss the following questions in their table groups:

✦ What do you know?
✦ Is there anything confusing? (words, phrases)
✦ What do you have to find out?

FIGURE 9-6.
Pedro used three different operations to represent the problem.

Christine circulated, listening in on students' discussions. She noticed that they were getting pretty good at identifying what they already knew and what they had to find out. However, in this problem, there were three words that were tricky for students: *Ukrainian*, *Mrs. Palmer*, and *collection*.

After a minute or so, Christine called the students back to attention and focused the discussion on the three tricky words. "On the count of three, let's all read the person's name in the story," Christine directed, pointing at the word in the story problem. "One, two, three!"

"Mrs. Palmer!"

"Reading people's names in word problems can be difficult," Christine noted. "What are some other words we can use if we can't read a person's name in a problem?"

"He!"

"Or she!"

"The woman, or man," Valerie added.

"Just skip it," Roxie advised.

"Those are all good suggestions," Christine acknowledged. She then described the meanings of the words *collection* and *Ukrainian* for the students and told them that sometimes there are hard words in a problem that students don't really need to know in order to solve it. To illustrate this, Christine modeled how to retell the word problem, making it easier to understand:

A woman has 54 eggs.
She gives each of her 6 grandchildren the same number of eggs.
How many eggs does she give each grandchild?

While Christine didn't have students do the retelling in this case, it is important for students to have direct experience and practice retelling problems in their own words.

Before sending students off to solve the problem, Christine helped them get started by asking them a few questions that were designed to push them to think about the elements in the problem and provide the support they would need for their drawings.

"If I'm going to make a picture of the problem, how many grandchildren will I draw?"

"Six!"

Christine drew six stick figures on the board. "And how many eggs does each grandchild get?" she asked. Christine's question was met with silence.

"We don't know yet, do we?" she told the students. "How can I get started drawing the eggs?"

"Give some eggs to each kid," Pedro suggested.

"Should they each get the same amount?" Christine probed. "Who can find the sentence in the word problem that tells us?" She gave the students a few seconds to reread the problem, and then she called on Amandita.

Amandita came up to the board and pointed to each word in the sentence as she read aloud, "She gives each of her grandchildren the same number of eggs."

Christine drew one egg next to each stick figure until all six had one egg each.

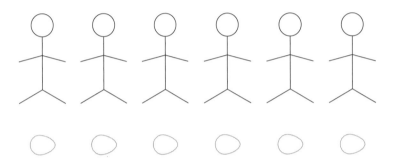

"Is that enough?" she asked.

"No!" the students chorused.

"What do I do now?" Christine asked the class.

"Keep giving them eggs until you pass out all fifty-four of them," Vic said.

Rather than finish the drawing for the class, Christine had the students complete the problem on their own and then had them share their solution strategies in a whole-class discussion. This brought closure to the two-day lesson. (See Figure 9–7.)

FIGURE 9-7. Valerie solved the problem using division, multiplication, and drawings.

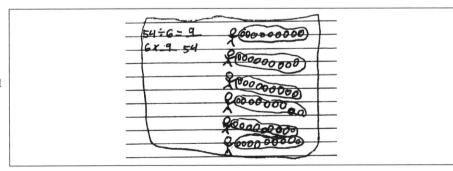

In the months following the lesson, Mrs. Gómez continued to use the strategies Christine had modeled to help her students make sense of and solve math word problems. She often began math class with a warm-up activity, posing a word problem and then using the following strategies with her students:

◆ Discuss what you know and what you have to find out.
◆ Talk about words or phrases that are confusing
◆ Find synonyms for difficult vocabulary and then retell the story problem.
◆ Draw a picture of the problem.
◆ Determine what the numbers in the problem represent.
◆ Identify and discuss words in the problem that have more than one meaning.
◆ Practice describing your solution strategies with a partner, in small groups, and with the whole class.
◆ Talk about what numbers and operation(s) will be used to solve the problem.

Activity Directions ◆ **Writing and Solving Multiplication and Division Word Problems**

Day 1

Minilesson Introducing Academic Language and Writing Math Stories

1. Elicit from students a list of things that come in groups and record their ideas on a class chart. For example:

Things That Come in Groups

2s	3s	4s	5s	6s	7s
pair of socks	sides on a triangle	wheels on a car	toes on one foot	sodas in one pack	days in a week
8s	**9s**	**10s**	**11s**	**12s**	
legs on an octopus	planets in our solar system	fingers on two hands	players on the field in a game of football	months in a year	

Make sure students understand grouping terms, such as *pair* and *dozen*.

2. Introduce the following sentence frames on a vocabulary chart and have students practice reading them, pausing for the blank spaces.

There are _____ _____.

Each _____ *has* _____ _____.

There are _____ _____ *altogether.*

Have students practice using the frames with information from the class chart.

3. Choose an item from one of the lists in the "Things That Come in Groups" chart (e.g., wheels on a car). Model writing a story:

There are 3 cars.
Each car has 4 wheels.
There are 12 wheels altogether.

Draw a picture that illustrates the story. Have students read aloud the story.

4. Direct students to choose something from the "Things That Come in Groups" chart and write a story using the sentence frames. Provide the following directions:

   a. Choose a number from the chart.
   b. Choose an item from the list.
   c. Think of how many of the item will be in your story.
   d. Write a story using the sentence frames.
   e. Draw a picture of your story.

5. Have students share their stories with classmates.

Writing Word Problems

1. Talk about what the term *unknown* means and provide a few examples of math sentences that include unknown numbers.

2. Model for the students how to write three different math word problems using the stories that they wrote.

   a. In each of the problems that they write, the unknown should be in a different place.
   b. Each math problem must end in a question.
   c. Each word problem should be written on a separate piece of paper.

Examples:

Story

There are 3 cars.
Each car has 4 wheels.
There are 12 wheels altogether.

Math Problem 1

There are 3 cars.
Each car has 4 wheels.
How many wheels altogether?

Math Problem 2

There are 3 cars.
There are 12 wheels altogether.
How many wheels on each car?

Math Problem 3

Each car has 4 wheels.
There are 12 wheels altogether.
How many cars are there?

3. Have each student write three math word problems from his story.

Day 2

Solving the Word Problems

1. Choose one of the student's math word problems and write it on the board. Direct the students to read aloud the problem with you.

2. Discuss the word problem with the students. Ask the following questions to help them think about the problem:

+ What do you know?
+ Is there anything confusing (words, phrases)?
+ What do you have to find out?

Add key vocabulary terms to chart as they come up.

3. Have students solve the problem.

4. Ask several students to explain how they solved the problem in a whole-class discussion. As they explain their thinking, provide needed support to assist students with language production.

5. Model for the students number sentences that describe the math word problems. For example:

Math Problem 1

There are 3 cars.
Each car has 4 wheels.
How many wheels altogether?
$3 \times 4 =$ _____

6. Have students exchange word problems to read and then solve.

7. Choose a few word problems from your math textbook or state test and have the class discuss and solve the problems together. Talk about confusing words and model how to retell problems with simpler language. Have students share their strategies for solving the problems.

How to Modify Math Lessons to Support English Language Learners 10

Education for English language learners (ELLs) in American classrooms has improved greatly over the last few decades as research has provided educators with strategies that make instruction more comprehensible. Teachers use visuals and manipulatives, capitalizing on the concrete nature of mathematics, to show students the subject matter content instead of just telling them about it. They simplify language so that ELLs can understand explanations more easily. They highlight key terms and often provide students with math journals or math vocabulary walls to be used as reference tools. All of this effort goes a long way toward making the teacher's lesson comprehensible to students whose native language is not English.

Comprehension is not a one-way street, however. It is not enough that the information is presented concretely and clearly. In order for a student to learn the concept being presented, she needs to interact with the information and make connections between what is already known and what is being learned. The learner then needs to test her new understandings by explaining what she has learned. All of these steps in the learning process—interacting with new knowledge, making connections, and testing understandings—happen through language. Moreover, they require that students produce language. It is at this point that the process often breaks down for the English learner. Without adequate linguistic support, an ELL cannot articulate her thinking. And if the concept happens to be a completely new one, the student's very *thinking* is compromised because humans use language to think.

Providing appropriate linguistic support involves consideration of each English language learner's proficiency level in English. Most English language development tests place students in one of various levels, typically described as beginning, intermediate, and advanced.

Within each level there is still a range of ability, and since students are generally tested only once a year, the accuracy of the score decreases as time passes and as the student progresses. Typically speaking, however, students at the beginning level respond nonverbally. They can still participate in tasks that demonstrate comprehension, such as identifying, matching, and categorizing, but only with strong visual and manipulative support. Students at the intermediate level can describe, explain, define, retell, summarize, compare, and contrast. While they need less physical support in terms of visual aids, they need grammatical support as they struggle to find the right words and order them into coherent sentences. ELLs at the advanced level can perform all of the higher-level functions that a native speaker can perform, giving opinions, justifying answers, negotiating, debating, persuading, and so on, but they lack the fine-tuning necessary for them to be considered a fluent speaker of English. While the specifics of language development may not be foremost in the mind of the teacher during a math lesson, it is during content instruction that the student is learning new information and has an authentic need to communicate his understandings. It is also during content instruction that the teacher has a need to assess student learning. Language must be the vehicle, and not the roadblock, for both of these goals.

This book contains a collection of carefully crafted lessons from several strands of mathematics. The lessons were selected because of their appropriateness across grade levels and because they introduce new concepts in each of the strands. They were designed with all of the different language proficiency levels in mind. While we hope these lessons allow your English language learners to experience more success in math, you, the classroom teacher, are our true audience for this book. We hope these lessons serve as models for modifying the key lessons you present throughout the course of the academic year. This chapter is designed to help you think about how to approach math instruction in order to best support students who are learning the English language and math simultaneously.

Selecting Math Lessons for Modification

Obviously, we are not suggesting that teachers rewrite their entire math curriculum. While new information is presented in most lessons, the information generally builds on concepts previously introduced. Once English language learners have a solid understanding of the basic concepts, adding new information is a less onerous process. Providing students with support in the development of the necessary language during introductory lessons will allow them to interact with the information, make the necessary connections, and test their thinking as the instruction continues. Some lessons provoke more thinking and communication than others. Therefore, we suggest you select the key lessons that introduce new concepts in each strand, chapter, or unit of study and lessons that require students to use new vocabulary and language structures to think and communicate. Modifying these lessons will ensure that ELLs benefit from your subsequent instruction.

Whether or not you decide to try adapting a lesson in the style we are modeling, the sample lessons will help you think about the role of language in the math classroom. Although it may be easy to find satisfaction in the deceptive nods that English learners give when asked if they understand a concept, it is much more reliable and informative to provide students with the opportunity and the language to articulate their understandings. The way teachers question ELLs can also affect the students' level of oral participation. If you ask questions with students' English proficiency levels in mind, they will be more likely to respond in a way that both solidifies their own understanding and allows you to assess their learning. The lesson vignettes in this book both address and provide examples of level-appropriate questioning. Additionally, focusing on the intricacies of English can help a teacher monitor whether or not the instruction is comprehensible. Multiple-meaning words and homophones can cause confusion for English language learners. A simple clarification of the intended meaning of a term can help them keep pace with the lesson. A list of multiple-meaning words used in mathematics is provided in the Appendix.

Modifying a Math Lesson

The lessons in this book have two goals, a math goal and a language goal. The math goal must be determined first; the language goal supports students' understanding of the math goal. Once you have identified what math content you are going to teach, think about what students would be able to say if they had met the math goal. For example, if the math goal involves learning about quadrilaterals, once students had met that goal they would be able to *describe* quadrilaterals and perhaps *compare and contrast* them with other geometric figures. If the math goal were that students solve a subtraction problem using an effective strategy that makes sense to them, then they would be able to *describe the sequence of steps* they used for solving the problem once they had met the goal. If the math goal states that students will learn about probability in dice games, then they will need to use language to *predict* the outcomes of future rolls of the dice. Each of these three math goals—learning about shapes, solving subtraction problems, and understanding probability—has a logical language goal (or goals) that accompanies it. In these cases the language goals are describing, comparing and contrasting, sequencing, and predicting.

Native English-speaking children are able to perform these language functions to articulate their math understanding when prompted with questions like "What do you know about quadrilaterals?" "What are your steps for solving a subtraction problem?" and "What do you predict I will roll next?" English language learners may understand the content of the lesson, but their inexperience with the language can keep them from articulating what they know. It is also possible that their struggles with the language of instruction lead them to partial or inaccurate understandings of the content. Until they verbalize their understandings, what they have learned or not learned remains a mystery to the teacher and may even be unclear to the students themselves. Choosing a language goal, or language function, that matches the math content goal makes the learning more observable to all.

Choosing the language goal is made easier by using the function chart in Figure 10–1. It lists twelve common functions of language and describes how they apply to the study of mathematics.

Determining Language Functions and Creating Sentence Frames

As there are purposes, or applications, for the various strands in mathematics, so are there purposes, or functions, for language. We use language to describe, to compare, to contrast, to predict, to categorize. Whether we are describing or categorizing in science, reading, social studies, or math, the sentence structure we use will be the same. For example, we might say that an element on the periodic table has a particular atomic weight, the main character in a story has a problem to solve, the United States has fifty states, or an algebraic expression has two variables. Each one of those describing statements uses the same basic sentence structure: _____ *has* _____. We call this structure a *frame*. Consider the function of cause and effect: If we add baking soda to vinegar, a gas will be produced; if the character in the story finds a comfortable bed, she will fall asleep in it; if the president vetoes the bill, Congress will have the votes to override the veto; if I divide the

Language Functions and Sentence Frames			
Function	**Beginning**	**Intermediate**	**Advanced**
Describing Nouns	A ____ has ____. A ____ is ____.	A ____ has ____, ____, and ____. A ____ is ____, ____, and ____.	A ____ might have ____ or ____, but it will always have ____.
Examples	A *square* has *four sides*.	A *triangle* has *three sides*, *three vertices*, and *no curves*.	A *polygon* might have *four sides* or *six sides*, but it will always have *straight sides*.
Categorizing	A ____ is a ____.	A ____ is a ____ because ____.	A ____ is a ____ because ____. It is not ____ because ____.
Examples	*Two* is an *even number*.	*Four* is an *even number* because *it can be divided into two equal groups*.	*Four* is an *even number* because *it can be divided into two equal groups*. It is not *odd* because *nothing is left over*.
Describing Location	The ____ is next to the ____.	The ____ is next to the ____ and below the ____.	The ____ is between the ____, beneath the ____, and to the right of ____.
Examples	The *square* is next to the *triangle*.	The *square* is next to the *triangle* and below the *hexagon*.	The *square* is between the *triangle and the rectangle*, beneath the *hexagon*, and to the right of the *circle*.
Comparing and Contrasting	A ____ has ____. A ____ is ____.	A ____ has ____, but a ____ has ____. ____ and ____ both have ____.	While a ____ and a ____ both have a ____, they are different because ____.
Examples	The *first number* has *three digits*.	The *second number* has *two digits*, but *the third number* has *four digits*.	While the *second number* and *the last number* both have *two digits*, they are different because *one is odd and one is even*.

FIGURE 10-1. Language functions and sentence frames.

Language Functions and Sentence Frames			
Function	**Beginning**	**Intermediate**	**Advanced**
Summarizing	A ___ has ___ and ___. ___ is ___ and ___.	___ always have ___. Some ___ are ___ and some are ___.	In conclusion, ___ have ___ and ___; however, ___ are not always ___.
Examples	A _fraction_ has a _numerator_ and a _denominator_.	_Fractions_ always have _numerators and denominators_. Some _numerators_ are _smaller than the denominators_ and some are _larger_.	In conclusion, _fractions_ have _numerators_ and _denominators_; however, the _numerators_ are not always _smaller than the denominators_.
Sequencing	First, ___. Second, ___.	First ___, and then ___.	After ___, ___. Before ___, ___.
Examples	First, _I counted the red blocks_. Second, _I counted the blue blocks_.	First, _I put the blocks in groups of ten_, and then _I counted them_.	After _I put the blocks in groups of ten_, _I counted them_.
Giving and Following Directions	Point to the ___. Draw a ___.	Put the ___ below the ___. Draw a ___ around the ___ and a ___ above the ___.	Put the ___ next to the ___, and you will form a ___.
Examples	Draw a _square_.	Put the _square_ below the _triangle_.	Put the _triangle_ next to the _other triangle_, and you will form a _rhombus_.
Hypothesizing	N/A	If ___, then ___ will ___.	When ___, the result will ___.
Examples	N/A	If _I divide 365 blocks by 10_, then I will have _some blocks left over_.	When _dividing an odd number by 10_, the result will _have a remainder_.
Predicting	The ___ will have ___.	I predict that ___ will ___.	I predict that ___ will ___ because ___.
Examples	I will _roll a 7_.	I predict that _I will roll a 7_.	I predict that _I will roll a 7_ because _I have rolled it more than any other number_.

Language Functions and Sentence Frames			
Function	**Beginning**	**Intermediate**	**Advanced**
Making Inferences	N/A	I can infer that ___.	I can infer that ___ because I know ___.
Examples	*N/A*	*I can infer that this is an addition problem.*	*I can infer that this is an addition problem because I know I need to find the total.*
Drawing Conclusions	N/A	I can conclude that ___.	I can conclude that ___ because ___ and ___.
Examples	*N/A*	*I can conclude that x is 5.*	*I can conclude that x is 5 because 2 times x is 10.*
Explaining Cause and Effect	The ___ is ___.	___ because ___.	___ caused ___ to ___.
Examples	*The answer is a negative number.*	*The answer is a negative number because we multiplied by a negative number.*	*Multiplying by a negative number caused the answer to be negative.*

FIGURE 10-1.
(*Continued*)

pizza in eighths, the four of us will get two pieces each. The frame is the same in all cases: *If _____, _____ will _____.* This is also true for skills like categorizing. In science you might say that helium, oxygen, and carbon dioxide are gases because they are made up of loosely connected molecules. In reading you would say Cinderella and Goldilocks are protagonists because they are the leading characters in literary works. In social studies certain countries are democracies because of their forms of government. And in math certain figures are polygons because they are closed and have three or more straight sides. In every case the language is supported by the same frame: *_____ is a _____ because _____.* These basic sentence structures can be powerful tools in the hands of students learning the English language. When structured appropriately, they are flexible enough to be useful in a variety of contexts. These frames allow such students to use the key vocabulary terms and put together complete thoughts, thoughts that can be connected, confirmed, rejected, revised, and understood.

Remembering that the students' language proficiency must be taken into account in order to provide the support that nudges students to the next level, teachers can design frames to create sentences that are increasingly more sophisticated. For example, if students are comparing and contrasting numbers or shapes in math, different English language learners will be ready to use language to think about and discuss their learning at various levels. Students with beginning levels of proficiency will be describing the numbers or shapes before they can compare and contrast them. They might use the frame _____ *has* _____ to express ideas like *A square has four sides* and *A triangle has three sides*. Such a limited frame would not serve intermediate-level students. They are ready to compare with frames like _____ *has* _____, *but* _____ *has* _____, composing sentences like *A square has four sides, but a triangle has three sides*. Advanced students are capable of refining their speech to include dependent clauses with frames: *While a* _____ *and a* _____ *are the same in that they* _____, *they are different because* _____. Using that frame in the same geometry lesson, an advanced ELL might declare, "While a square and a triangle are the same in that they are both polygons, they are different because they have a different number of sides and vertices." The goal of the frames is twofold: to provide ELLs the linguistic support they need to learn about and demonstrate their knowledge of the math content while pushing their English language abilities to the next level of proficiency. The frames also provide practical applications for the language students are learning during their English language development lessons.

While the frames may seem abstract outside the context of the math lesson, English language learners almost immediately see the usefulness of them because they help students out with the hard parts of the language. Before students are asked to use a sentence frame, they learn key vocabulary terms that they can place in the frame to begin to talk about their learning. Frames are also introduced with familiar math concepts before they are used with new information. For instance, students might describe common objects using the descriptive frames before they describe polygons. Once students understand the concept of the frame, they often try to use frames above their proficiency level, realizing that the frames allow them to produce much more complicated sentences than they would ordinarily use. The goal is not to create a fill-in-the-blank sentence that has correct and incorrect answers; rather the frames should provide a scaffold that English learners can use to construct and discuss their thoughts.

Refer to the chart in Figure 10–1 to determine the language function that students will need to perform in order to articulate the particular math knowledge you want them to learn. Will they be describing geometric shapes, categorizing numbers, comparing the lengths of objects, predicting the outcomes of a probability game, or drawing conclusions about a set of data?

Once you have determined the function, choose frames that meet the linguistic needs of your students, whether they are beginning, intermediate, or advanced. Mold the frames to fit the particular lesson. Consider the number of blanks necessary for your frame. For example, *A _____ has _____* is effective for describing a circle, but *_____ have _____, _____, and _____* might work better for describing polygons. What verb tense would be most natural? Do you want students to articulate their thinking in the past, present, past, future, or conditional tense? When predicting, the future tense is the most logical because you are making educated guesses about an event that has not yet happened. When asking students to sequence the steps they used to solve a math word problem, setting the frames in the past tense makes more sense. The conditional tense is ideal for hypothesizing: *If I placed the triangles side by side, the result* would be *a quadrilateral.* Is the subject of the frame singular or plural? The answer to this question affects the article and the verb in the frame. If students are describing a singular object, say a rectangle, they will need a frame designed for a single object: *A _____ has _____.* If students are describing a series of numbers, they will need a frame designed for multiple items: *_____, _____, and _____ have _____.* Once you have determined your frame, try it out yourself several times to make sure it is flexible enough to articulate many different examples. If slight modifications are necessary, for example, using both singular and plural subjects, be prepared to alter the frame as the students are using it.

Determining Key Vocabulary

Most math books now include a set of key terms for each lesson. This is a great place to start determining what words English language learners will need to know, but it is by no means an exhaustive list. Since math knowledge is cumulative, students who have spent less time learning in English may not know the previously taught terms that are the foundation for a particular lesson. In addition to content terms, consider some of the language in your frames that may be unfamiliar. For example, if you are asking students to predict, do they know what *predict* means? Are there any other terms that you want students to be able to use during the lesson that you haven't heard them use with confidence in general conversation? If a term is not in the students' oral vocabulary, directly teaching it might be a good idea.

Once you have determined the key vocabulary for the lesson, give some thought as to when to teach each term. Some of the words must be taught at the beginning of the lesson in order for students to follow along. Other words will not appear until partway through the lesson, and it may be more logical to teach them at that time. For example, teaching the word *triangle* would be important to start off a lesson on the different types of triangles. Teaching the words *isosceles* and *equilateral* may not be necessary until after students have done some experimentation, made some comparisons, and taken some measurements. The students will retain the meanings of only those words they have an actual need for. Anticipating that need and providing the vocabulary at that moment will have the most impact on student learning.

Designing a Minilesson to Introduce the Mathematical Language

Learning math and language at the same time is a cognitively demanding endeavor. In order to support English language learners, design a minilesson that will allow students to try out the frames on familiar math material before they are faced with the academic demands of the grade-level lesson. The plans in this book provide models for such lessons. When we wanted students to learn and articulate the characteristics of polygons, we had them practice using the sentence frames and key vocabulary to describe everyday objects, like quarters, windows, and clocks. When we wanted students to say whether an outcome would be likely or unlikely during a probability experiment, we first had them practice using those terms to describe the likelihood of real-life events: what the weather would be like, whether or not they would have homework, and when they would eat lunch. Allowing students to practice the frames with familiar concepts helps them internalize the structures, builds their confidence in volunteering answers, and prepares them to be successful during the math lesson.

Building in Opportunities for Talk

Language goals, sentence frames, and key vocabulary are useful to the students only if they have opportunities to talk during the lesson. All of these linguistic supports are meant to scaffold students' learning during instruction as well as allow them to showcase their learning after instruction. Arguably the most important role of the sentence frames is to help the students formulate their thinking as they are learning the math content. That thinking must occur throughout the lesson in order for the students to keep pace with the instruction.

Building in opportunities for structured and guided talk throughout the lesson will promote both thinking and learning. These opportunities for student talk will also allow you to redirect students if misconceptions or confusions arise. Consider using any or all of the following strategies for facilitating student talk in your lesson.

Think, Pair, Share

After each meaningful chunk of instruction, provide students with time to think about what they have learned, pair up with a partner to discuss their ideas, and then share their ideas with the class. Scaffold all three of these activities by posting, explaining, modeling, and encouraging the use of the sentence frames.

Repeating and Rewording

During the presentation of a lesson, students are exposed to many important concepts. Often these concepts build on one another to achieve the math goal of the lesson. Achievement of that math goal can be improved if teachers hold students responsible for each important chunk of learning throughout the lesson. One way to accomplish this is to ask students to either repeat or reword key concepts as they are presented. While repeating may not seem like a high-level task, it is much more active than simply listening to the concepts as they are presented. Rewording key information encourages students to express a new concept in their own language, a language we know they understand. Students can repeat or reword statements made by the teacher or by other students. The teacher can also repeat or reword statements made by students in order to emphasize or question information.

Partner Work and Group Work

When directing students to explore with manipulatives, practice a skill, solve problems, conduct an experiment, draw a figure, create a chart, or compare numbers, have them work in pairs. Working with a partner creates the need for communication. Communication requires the thoughtful use of language. This is yet another opportunity for students to use the sentence frames and the key vocabulary to build their content knowledge and their language ability.

Supportive Questioning

Probably the most common way for teachers to invite student participation in a lesson is through questioning. While inquiring and checking for understanding are natural parts of teaching, simply asking questions may not elicit the desired participation from all English language learners. Students with advanced proficiency levels in English may respond to questions, as would any native English speaker, yet students with intermediate and beginning proficiency levels may need more support in order to produce a response. When asked a question such as "What steps did you use to solve the problem?" students with intermediate and beginning proficiency levels must produce so much language just to structure their answer (language to sequence their steps, past-tense verbs, math vocabulary) that they might choose not to answer at all.

A teacher can provide support, however, to elicit responses and improve the participation of students with lower levels of English proficiency. When questioning beginning-level students, ask a question or provide a prompt that requires a physical response ("Point to the square." "Touch the even number.") or a question with a yes-or-no answer ("Is one line segment longer than the other?"). When asking short-answer questions, build the answers into the questions for additional support: "Is this a circle or a square?" "Is the number odd or even?" "Should we divide or multiply?"

Students with intermediate levels of proficiency in English need less support to understand and respond to questions from the teacher, but carefully crafted questions can improve the quality of both their responses and their English. For example, instead of asking an intermediate-level student, "What do you predict will happen?" you might phrase your question this way: "What color do you predict we will select if we pull another block out of the bag?" The second question models the structure of a well-crafted answer: "I predict we will select red if we pull another block out of the bag." Compare that with the response more likely from the first question: "Red."

Questioning students lets teachers know what students have learned. Answering questions lets students test, confirm, or modify their own understandings. None of these goals can be met unless the questions are structured in a way that produces a response from the students. In addition to improving student participation, thoughtful questions can improve the quality of the students' responses.

Explaining Thinking

When teaching the lesson, make sure to prompt students to explain their thinking. When a student provides either a correct or an incorrect answer to a question, the more important information is how the student arrived at that answer. The correct answer may have been a lucky guess. It may also have been the result of good mathematical reasoning and problem solving that could serve as an example for other students. There is no way of knowing unless we ask students to explain their thinking. Likewise, an incorrect answer may have been the result of a careless mistake or it may represent complete confusion on the part of the student. Asking students to explain their thinking makes the learning process more transparent. Students with beginning levels of proficiency in English may not yet have the language necessary to explain their thinking. Providing manipulatives or visuals so that such students can *show* their thinking can give you insight into their learning.

Writing About Thinking

English language development involves four domains: listening, speaking, reading, and writing. Once students can verbalize their ideas about the math content using the sentence frames and the key vocabulary, they are ready to stretch to the next level and write down their ideas. Their writing is scaffolded by the frames as well as by the talk.

How We Develop Lessons

When designing lessons for English language learners, we follow a few important steps. The process is recursive, of course, as we return to particular sections of each lesson to revise our plan and make it as coherent as possible. Following is a sample of how we designed one particular lesson, *Round Things* (see Chapter 7).

Identify a math goal.

We selected the math goal of comparing the circumferences of circles with their diameters and drawing conclusions about the relationship between the two measurements because it is a concept that is introduced in upper-elementary grades and then built upon in future grades. This important concept is the type of basic knowledge that English language learners will need in order to be successful in their future math studies.

Choose a language goal that serves the math goal.

Knowing that students would be exploring the relationship between two different measurements of circles, we determined that the language goals would be for students to compare and contrast and to then draw conclusions.

Determine key vocabulary.

Many of the terms we introduced in this lesson came straight from the adopted math curriculum, like *diameter, circumference,* and *radius.* We chose other words in order to meet the specific needs of ELLs. We knew that comparing and contrasting involved the use of comparative adjectives, so we introduced *longer, shorter, bigger,* and *smaller.* We also knew that since the mathematical relationship between a circle's circumference and its diameter involves the number pi, we had better introduce the terms *about, around,* and *approximately* in order to help students deal with the inexactness of the numbers. Since we wanted students to be able to describe what they did with the numbers to determine their relationship, we added the terms *multiply* and *divide* to the list.

Design sentence frames.

This lesson was designed for an upper-elementary classroom that included native English-speaking students and English language learners at the beginning, intermediate, and advanced levels. We used the function chart to guide us as we created frames that would support students in this particular lesson. We decided that the beginning-level students could talk about the circumference and the diameter of a circle using this structure: _____ is _____. _____ is _____. We wanted the intermediate students to use comparative language, so we modified the frames for them: _____ is _____ than _____. _____ is _____ times _____ than _____. The advanced students would need frames that would help them make more complex statements: _____ is about/around/approximately _____ of _____. _____ is about/around/approximately _____ times _____ than _____. We practiced using these frames with the content from the lesson until we were satisfied that they were usable and supportive.

Design a minilesson to introduce the academic language.

We designed a small activity in which students would use the sentence frames to compare and contrast things they were already familiar with before diving into the content of circumferences and diameters. In the beginning of the lesson students are asked to compare and contrast line segments and numbers so that they will have the opportunity to use the frames to express ideas they are comfortable with and confident about. We also introduce the key vocabulary at this point, with the exception of the more technical geometry terms, so that students are equipped with useful language before they take the plunge into new learning.

Build in opportunities for talk.

We begin providing students with opportunities to talk in the minilesson. They are asked to compare the line segments and the numbers with partners. After presenting the frames, we ask them to practice using the frames with a partner, and then we call on various students to share their statements with the class. At the conclusion of the minilesson, we direct students to share their thinking in small groups and with the class as a whole.

The main lesson involves students working with partners, so talk is a necessity. Students are also required to document their discoveries on construction paper, using the key vocabulary to label their findings. As the students work, the lesson plan directs the teacher to monitor their progress by asking specific questions regarding each term. This reinforces the vocabulary and allows students to practice using the sentence frames. Once the exploration phase ends, students are asked to discuss their findings with their partners, again using the frames and the key vocabulary. This talk culminates with a class discussion about the relationship between a circle's circumference and its diameter.

Design a writing prompt.

We end the lesson by asking students to write about their understanding of the relationship between a circle's circumference and its diameter. This is an individual assignment that serves as a method for us to check for understanding. The frames are available to students as they write because we are assessing their math knowledge, not their language proficiencies.

Now You Try It

Identify a math goal.

Select a math goal for your lesson. Remember that you are looking for key concepts that build foundational knowledge, promote critical thinking, and/or involve an extensive use of language.

Choose a language goal that serves the math goal.

Once you have selected an appropriate math lesson for modification, decide what language students will need to articulate their learning. Think about what they will say throughout the lesson to demonstrate that they are learning the concept. What language function will they need to perform? Will they need to describe, categorize, compare, contrast, summarize, sequence, give directions, hypothesize, predict, make inferences, draw conclusions, or establish cause and effect?

Determine the key vocabulary.

What math terms will be introduced in this lesson? What previously introduced terms and everyday words are still unfamiliar to the ELLs in your class? What multiple-meaning words will appear in the lesson? Are there any other essential words that might cause confusion? List these terms and decide when in the lesson you will introduce each one.

Design sentence frames for multiple proficiency levels.

Use the "Language Functions and Sentence Frames" chart (Figure 10–1) to find sample frames that match the language function you chose. Work with the frames until they fit the needs of your lesson. Determine what verb tense would sound most natural. Decide how many blanks to include in each frame and where to put them. Design frames that will fit the various English proficiency levels represented in your class and will allow students to verbalize the key lesson concepts. Record the frames on chart paper or sentence strips.

Design a minilesson to introduce the language.

Once you have created your sentence frames, design a brief lesson in which the students can practice the frames with familiar math content. For example, if the students will be comparing large or awkward numbers (decimals, fractions, negative integers), have them practice using the frames with smaller, less cumbersome numbers. If students will be summarizing the steps used to solve complicated computational problems, plan a lesson in which they can use the sentence frames to summarize the steps they took to solve a more basic problem. Remember that the goal of this minilesson is to familiarize the students with the sentence frames so that during the main lesson they can devote their thinking to the math content.

Build in opportunities for talk.

Beginning with the minilesson and continuing throughout the main math lesson, build in opportunities for students to talk to one another and to you about their learning. These opportunities should include discussions that build background and allow students to make connections to what they already know about the topic, exploratory talk that encourages students to hypothesize or make predictions about the new concept, clarifying conversations in which students explain what they think they understand about the new concept, and concluding conversations in which students solidify their new knowledge. Also, spend time crafting questions to ensure the participation of students with different proficiency levels. Refer to the suggestions in "Building in Opportunities for Talk" (see page 173) to ensure there is a variety of activities that will keep students engaged and participating.

Design a writing prompt to conclude the lesson.

While talk allows students to explore their knowledge in a relatively nonthreatening manner, it does not necessarily provide the teacher with information on each individual student's learning. In order to assess what students have learned both mathematically and linguistically from the lesson, design an open-ended question or prompt and ask students to commit their ideas to paper at the end of the lesson.

Lesson Template

Math Goal

_____

_____

Language Goal

_____

_____

Key Vocabulary

_____   _____   _____

_____   _____   _____

_____   _____   _____

_____   _____   _____

Materials

_____   _____   _____

_____   _____   _____

Sentence Frames That Support the Language Goal

    Beginning:

    _____

    _____

    Intermediate:

    _____

    _____

    Advanced:

    _____

    _____

Activity Directions for the Minilesson (including opportunities to talk)

1.
2.
3.

Activity Directions for the Main Lesson (including opportunities to talk)

1.
2.
3.
4.
5.

Writing Prompt

FIGURE 10-2.
Lesson
template.

Refer students to the sentence frames for support with this activity. Encourage students to draw what they learned if they are not yet comfortable expressing their ideas in writing.

Simplify the information using a lesson template.

The template in Figure 10–2 is designed to help you capture all of the information you have been considering while designing your lesson. This is the type of document you could save for math instruction in future years, share with colleagues who are looking for ways to support their English language learners, or even modify to use with other subject areas like science and social studies.

Reflecting on the Modifications

When we wrote the math lessons detailed in this book, the three of us worked together to design a lesson and then taught the lesson several times in order to revise it. We observed each other's lessons and took notes on the teaching and the learning, and then we met to debrief each lesson. Reflecting on our planning and on our teaching led us to many of the insights we have shared in this book. We learned what Farrell (2003) meant by saying that experience alone is not as important as reflecting on that experience.

Take the necessary time after teaching a math lesson you have modified to reflect on how successful the lesson was. Did the ELLs in your class meet the math goal? Did they meet the language goal? Did they participate more than they normally do in math lessons? Were the frames you created appropriate for the lesson? Did you use too many frames or too few? What changes would have made the lesson more successful?

The work of modifying math lessons to not only make them comprehensible but also provide language support to help English learners think about new concepts, experiment with their knowledge, and solidify their understanding is not easy. This is the type of work, however, that allows English language learners to fully participate in their learning community and fully benefit from your teaching.

11 Frequently Asked Questions

1. The ideas presented in this book just seem like good teaching. Why is it targeted for English language learners (ELLs)?

While it is true that all learners will benefit from the strategies presented in this book, the methods are essential for ELLs to have access to the core math curriculum. Without the use of explicit vocabulary instruction, visual aids, and opportunities to communicate during math lessons, ELLs would have difficulty understanding the material presented, whether verbal or written. This could create huge gaps or misunderstandings in the math concepts presented. Try to imagine yourself learning new content about teaching in a second language. It would be essential for the instructor to provide scaffolds for you to make sense of the material he was presenting. Again, while the native speakers would likely benefit from the scaffolding, the scaffolds would be essential for *your* learning.

A second, even more compelling reason this book is targeted for ELLs is the focus on the development of the English language needed to participate fully in the math lessons. The implementation of the sentence frames provides ELLs with linguistic support so they can communicate mathematically and deepen their learning. This, in turn, provides us with opportunities for assessment and helps us make pivotal instructional decisions for our students.

2. Do the strategies in this book work for all ELLs regardless of their native language?

The strategies in this book will be effective for helping all ELLs, whatever their native language. Most teachers find that students who have strong oral language skills in their primary language have an easier time acquiring a second language, in this case, English. All ELLs benefit from direct, explicit instruction in English; simply being in an English environment is not enough. Hence, the strategies in this book will help your students learn math content and acquire English, regardless of their primary language.

3. What if I have only a few ELLs in my class and they are all at different language levels? Will this affect my native English-speaking students?

This is a common concern, because many teachers are in this exact situation. We have found that it is very appropriate to teach these lessons to the whole group and that the majority of students benefit from the additional attention to English. For example, native English-speaking students tend to use the advanced frames, which have more complex academic language than they are used to using. Although they may have been able to explain their mathematical thinking without the support of the frames, native English speakers are now acquiring a more sophisticated way of doing so. ELLs at different proficiency levels seem to self-regulate their use of the frames, which is why all students are introduced to and practice all of the frames regardless of their level of English proficiency. Providing all students access to all of the frames increases their level of metalinguisitic reflection (their thinking about their language use) and helps them mediate their language learning. However, in some classrooms where the makeup of students is extremely diverse (high achievers, ELLs, resource), small groups may be the best way to teach the minilessons.

4. I have a student in my class who barely speaks any English. What can I do to support the student?

It is not uncommon to have students in your classroom who are at the very beginning stages of learning English. Students often come directly from their home countries speaking little or no English. This can create quite a challenge for a teacher trying to ensure that the newcomers have equal access to content.

One fifth-grade teacher used a number of strategies to assist a newcomer to her class when teaching a lesson on adding and subtracting fractions. The students had been learning how to find the least common multiple of two numbers as a way to add and subtract fractions that did not share the same denominator. José was a student who had just moved to the United States from Mexico; he spoke very little English. When the students were given a word problem that required them to add $\frac{1}{3} + \frac{1}{6}$, the classroom teacher supported José in several different ways.

First, she had José sit next to Eduardo, a native Spanish speaker with an advanced level of English. Eduardo was able to translate the word problem for José, thereby using a student's primary language as a teaching resource.

To provide students with a visual representation of fractions, the teacher had them make fraction strips in class. José had access to these concrete materials in case he needed them to model the problem.

Finally, the teacher had some background information about José as a learner. She knew that he came to the classroom with strengths in mathematics, particularly with computational procedures. So to remind the class about how to find the least common multiple of three and six, she called on José. He was able to recite the common multiples of the two numbers using very little language. This served to highlight his math strengths and build his confidence.

5. My English language learners seem to struggle more in math than my other students. Should I adjust my expectations for these students?

The adjustments need to occur in the presentation of material and not in what is expected of students. It may seem that ELLs struggle more in math compared with your native English speakers. This, however, does not indicate that they are in any way less capable than other students or that you should lower your expectations for them. What you are witnessing may be a language barrier that is preventing your ELLs from demonstrating their understanding of the material. Language difficulties may be masking the good mathematical thinking that ELLs are capable of and could possibly express in their primary language.

We need to adjust our instruction to find out what our students know and value the experiences they do have. Once we know more about our students, then we can design instruction to make sure we are providing them with an equitable education and allowing them access to the entire curriculum that native English-speaking students receive on a daily basis. It is our professional obligation to modify our lessons so that all students meet grade-level standards.

6. What is academic language and how is it different from social language?

Academic language is defined as the language used in schools. But what exactly does that mean? It is the language that we use in formal learning environments connected to specific subject matter. For example, we may direct students to *summarize* a story, make a *causal statement* about the Civil War, or *draw conclusions* about a scientific experiment. These cognitive functions are correlated to a certain type of language structure that students need to understand, whether material is presented orally or in text, and must be able to produce orally and in writing. In addition to the text structure, word order (syntax) and vocabulary (topic-specific terms related to a subject) are also part of academic language. Acquiring academic language is key to success in schools and access to higher education.

In regard to the math lessons in this book, the language goals listed for each lesson are the language functions that we identified as the key cognitive tasks that students would be doing in the lessons. For example, when students have to predict the probability of sums in *Roll Two Dice* (see Chapter 5), the academic language they will need to know to be able to fully participate in the lesson is that for making predictions and drawing conclusions, such as *I predict that _____ will win because _____* or *If we play* Roll Two Dice *again, _____ is/are likely to win because _____* and specific vocabulary terms such as *likely, unlikely, predict, sums, most,* and *least.* Academic language is usually related to content and often highly decontextualized, which increases the chance for difficulty in understanding and applying it.

In contrast, social language is easier to acquire because it is often used in everyday interactions surrounding common activities and topics. We don't always need specific terminology when speaking in social situations since we can usually refer to the topic at hand, such as the show on TV or the game on the playground. We also can use other ways to communicate besides language, such as gestures, phrases, and colloquial words, in order to participate in discussions. In addition, because of the frequency with which we interact in informal situations, there are many opportunities to practice the language of socializing or everyday activities. Many times our ELLs seem very adept with English, but we should always be checking to see whether their fluency is with the social use of English or the demands of academic English.

7. Some of my ELLs are really good at computation. Math is the only time that they can be successful without having to speak English. Why the emphasis on talking during math class?

Providing time for productive talk in math class can improve students' computation abilities. Being good at computation requires the kind of flexibility in thinking that enables a student to choose an efficient strategy for a particular problem to yield a correct answer. In order for students to become flexible problem solvers, they must be aware that numerous strategies for finding an answer may exist. By participating in mathematical discussions, students become aware of a variety of computation strategies and get a chance to develop their English language skills at the same time.

In addition, many concepts in math involve noncomputational, critical thinking. Since teachers instruct using language and students learn and think through language, devoting time to discussions during math instruction is essential for developing mathematical knowledge. Finally, without providing a forum for students to discuss their mathematical thinking, we might make incorrect assumptions about the learning that is occurring during math time. To be effective math instructors, we must assess thinking and learning, and language is the medium through which we do that.

8. This book is for grades 3 through 5. Will the lessons, as written, work for all three grades?

This book is meant to demonstrate how to modify math lessons for the ELLs in your class and to provide some examples in the various math strands for intermediate- to upper-elementary grades. We suggest drawing on these lessons as guides, using the ones in the book as highly structured activities that you can try out and implement immediately with your students. Then, after experimenting with the lessons and strategies, you can begin to apply the strategies in the book to modify your own math lessons. Moreover, you know your students and your math curriculum best, so you will be the most adept in deciding if the lesson content is appropriate to your group of students and in determining the amount of adjustments you'll have to make.

9. I noticed that you spend time practicing the sentence frames orally before beginning the math lessons. I'm worried about time. Is the oral practice really necessary?

One of the things that we know about teaching is that there never seems to be enough time for everything we would like to do in a day. Adding more to our day just seems impossible. We need to constantly scrutinize our schedules to make sure we are maximizing learning time for our students. In this case, we do need to make the time for oral language practice before jumping into a math lesson. If students do not get to practice the frames in the minilessons with content that is less cognitively demanding, they will not refer to them at all when they are engaged in the more taxing math lesson. Building in time for practice encourages students to use the academic language that will be required of them in the math lesson and gives them opportunities to receive feedback on that language. Once they feel some ownership of the language, they will be more likely to apply it later on. It is important that oral language practice has a meaningful purpose, and the minilessons provide that authentic setting to rehearse the new language while reviewing or introducing key mathematical ideas. The time invested in oral language practice prior to the lesson will improve student learning and thereby save time that would have been spent reteaching the math concepts later on.

10. Do students get confused when there are too many sentence frames? How many sentence frames should I present at a time?

Students absolutely can become confused with too many sentence frames and frames that are not presented well. Ideally, we would suggest one sentence frame for the key mathematical concept, differentiated for all the levels in your class. To visually differentiate the frames, we color-code them so that it is easy for students to distinguish one from another. Students respond well to the color-coding and it also allows them to self-monitor the language they use by experimenting with different levels and determining which ones they are comfortable with and which frames allow them to challenge themselves.

Additional considerations when deciding how many frames to present are the levels of English proficiency you are working with. As you may have noticed in the *Round Things* lesson (Chapter 7), the ELLs in that class were only intermediate and advanced; therefore, those were the only frames introduced. You also need to think about what you expect your students to produce orally or in writing in order to demonstrate their comprehension of the mathematical concepts. You need to define the key concepts you want to assess in their learning. For example, in the *Round Things* lesson, we had students make predictions about and make comparisons between the diameter and the circumference of a circle. Instead of providing the students with both sets of written sentence frames, we chose to just orally present the sentence stem "I predict . . ." and present written sentence frames for comparing, the key component we wanted to assess. A final point is your students' experience with the sentence frames and mathematical concepts associated with them. Your students may be familiar with the language used in prediction; if so, there's no need to reteach those frames. We suggest posting the frames previously taught in your room for students to use in future lessons.

11. It's sometimes difficult to tell the difference between a sentence frame for intermediate ELLs and one for advanced ELLs. For example, the following frames seem equally difficult:

Intermediate

> The _____ is/has _____, but the _____
> is/has _____. Both have _____.

Advanced

> While the _____ and the _____ both have
> _____, _____ _____.

It can be difficult to distinguish what makes one frame more advanced than another, but that is where a closer examination of the English language comes into play. To a native English speaker, the English language is very transparent. We use it effortlessly and without much thought to the grammar and construction of our sentences. With a sharper eye and ear to English and the help of resources on linguistics and English language development standards, we can become more adept at creating frames appropriate for different levels of proficiency.

Let's take a look at these two frames in more detail. While both sentences are similar in that they both have present-tense verbs and both use the word *both* in them, they differ in the complexity of their structure. The first frame is a compound sentence composed of two simple sentences. In order to express their mathematical understanding, students plug in the characteristics to compare and contrast two figures. The language for comparison is scaffolded for them so they can participate in the math lesson and demonstrate their comprehension of the concepts without becoming mired in the language. The second, more advanced frame begins with a dependent clause, making it a complex sentence, and requires students to have the language to complete the second half of the sentence on their own. It is more open-ended and assumes a higher level of familiarity with English in order to explain how the two figures compare.

Appendix

Multiple-Meaning Words in Mathematics

acute
altitude
base
change
chord
closed
composite
coordinate
combination
count
degree
difference
digit
edge
even
expression
face
factor
fair
figure
foot
formula
function
identity
improper
inequality

inscribe
intersection
irrational
key
left
mass
mean
median
multiple
negative
net
obtuse
odd
open
operation
origin
period
plane
plot
point
power
prime
product
proper
property
range

rational
ray
reflection
relative
right
root
round
ruler
scale
segment
set
side
similar
slide
solution
space
sum
table
term
times
translation
union
unit
value
volume
yard

Blackline Masters

Identifying and Describing Polygons Cards

Identifying and Describing Polygons
Record Sheet

Draw a polygon. Then write everything you know about polygons.

_____

_____

_____

_____

_____

_____

_____

From *Supporting English Language Learners in Math Class, Grades 3–5* by Rusty Bresser, Kathy Melanese, and Christine Sphar. © 2009 Math Solutions Publications.

Roll Two Dice Record Sheet

2	3	4	5	6	7	8	9	10	11	12

Finish Line

Round Things Record Sheet

Object	Diameter	Circumference
1.		
2.		
3.		
4.		
5.		

What do you notice about the relationship between the diameter and the circumference of the circles?

_____

_____

_____

_____

_____

Lesson Template

Math Goal

_____

_____

Language Goal

_____

_____

Key Vocabulary

_____   _____   _____

_____   _____   _____

_____   _____   _____

_____   _____   _____

Materials

_____   _____   _____

_____   _____   _____

Sentence Frames to Support Language Goal
    Beginning: _____
    Intermediate: _____
    Advanced: _____

Activity Directions for the Minilesson (including opportunities to talk)
1.
2.
3.

Activity Directions for the Main Lesson (including opportunities to talk)
1.
2.
3.
4.
5.

Writing Prompt

_____

_____

From *Supporting English Language Learners in Math Class, Grades 3–5* by Rusty Bresser, Kathy Melanese, and Christine Sphar. © 2009 Math Solutions Publications.

References

California Department of Education. *The Language Census Data, 2006–2007*. www.cde.ca.gov.

Carrasquilo, Angela, and Philip Segan, ed. 1998. *The Teaching of Reading in Spanish to the Bilingual Student*. 2d ed. Mahwah, NJ: Lawrence Erlbaum.

Chapin, Suzanne H., and Art Johnson. 2006. *Math Matters: Understanding the Math You Teach, Grades K–8*. 2d ed. Sausalito, CA: Math Solutions Publications.

Chapin, Suzanne H., Catherine O'Connor, and Nancy Canavan Anderson. 2003. *Classroom Discussions: Using Math Talk to Help Students Learn, Grades 1–6*. Sausalito, CA: Math Solutions Publications.

Cobb, Paul, Ada Boutfi, Kay McClain, and Joy Whitenack. 1997. "Reflective Discourse and Collective Reflection." *Journal for Research in Mathematics Education* 28 (3): 258–77.

Cummins, Jim. 2004. "Supporting ESL Students in Learning the Language of Mathematics." In *Mathematics: Every Student Learns, Grade 1*. New York: Scott Foresman Addison Wesley.

Dutro, Susana, and California Reading and Literature Project. 2003. *A Focused Approach to Frontloading English Language Instruction for Houghton Mifflin Reading, K–6*. Santa Cruz: Toucan Ed.

Dutro, Susana, and Carrol Moran. 2003. "Rethinking English Language Instruction: An Architectural Approach." In *English Learners: Reaching the Highest Levels of English Literacy*, ed. Gilbert G. García (227–58). Newark, DE: International Reading Association.

Farrell, Thomas S. C. 2003. *Reflective Practices in Action: 80 Reflection Breaks for Busy Teachers*. Thousand Oaks, CA: Corwin.

Fillmore, L. W., and Catherine E. Snow. 2000. "What Teachers Need to Know About Language." www.cal.org/ericll/teachers.pdf.

Full Option Science System (FOSS) Series. 1993. Berkeley: Lawrence Hall of Science, University of California.

García, Gilbert G., ed. 2003. *English Learners: Reaching the Highest Level of English Literacy*. Newark, DE: International Reading Association.

Garrison, Leslie. 1997. "Making the NCTM's Standards Work for Emergent English Speakers." *Teaching Children Mathematics* 4 (3): 132–38.

Hiebert, James, Thomas P. Carpenter, Elizabeth Fennema, Karen C. Fuson, Diana Wearne, and Hanlie Murray. 1997. *Making Sense: Teaching and Learning Mathematics with Understanding*. Portsmouth, NH: Heinemann.

Hiebert, James, and Diana Wearne. 1993. "Instructional Tasks, Classroom Discourse, and Students' Learning in Second-Grade Arithmetic." *American Educational Research Journal* 30 (2): 393–425.

Hill, Jane D., and Kathleen M. Flynn. 2006. *Classroom Instruction That Works with English Language Learners*. Alexandria, VA: Association of Supervision and Curriculum Development.

Honig, Bill, Linda Diamond, and Linda Gutlohn. 2007. *Teaching Reading Sourcebook*. Berkeley, CA: Consortium on Reading Excellence (CORE).

Khisty, Lena L. 1995. "Making Inequality: Issues of Language and Meanings in Mathematics Teaching with Hispanic Students." In *New Directions for Equity in Mathematics Education*, ed. Walter G. Secada, Elizabeth Fennema, and Linda B. Adajian (279–98). New York: Cambridge University Press.

Krashen, Stephen D., and Tracy D. Terrell. 1983. *The Natural Approach: Language Acquisition in the Classroom*. Hayward, CA: Alemany.

Kress, Jacqueline E. 1993. *The ESL Teacher's Book of Lists*. West Nyack, NY: Center for Applied Research in Education.

Lampert, Magdalene. 1990. "When the Problem Is Not the Question and the Solution Is Not the Answer: Mathematical Knowing and Teaching." *American Educational Research Journal* 27 (1): 29–63.

McGraw-Hill Mathematics, California Edition. 2002. New York: McGraw-Hill School Division.

McLaughlin, B. 1985. *Second-Language Acquisition in Childhood: Vol. 2: School-Age Children*. 2d ed. Hillsdale, NJ: Lawrence Erlbaum.

National Assessment of Educational Progress (NAEP). 2007. National Assessment of Educational Progress. 2007. http://nationsreportcard.gov/math_2007/m0015.asp.

National Clearinghouse for English Language Acquisition. 2007. http://gwu.edu/policy/states/reports/statedata/2005LEP/GrowingLEP0506.pdf.

National Council of Teachers of Mathematics (NCTM). 2000. *Principles and Standards for School Mathematics.* Reston, VA: NCTM.

Schlein, Miriam. 1996. *More Than One.* New York: Scholastic.

Teachers of English to Speakers of Other Languages (TESOL). 2006. "Access the Latest Standards Documents." Accessed November 1, 2007. www.tesol.org/s_tesol/seccss.asp?CID=281&DID=1771.

U.S. Department of Education. 2000. "Getting Ready for College Early: A Handbook for Parents of Students in Middle and Junior High School Years." Accessed November 1, 2007. www.ed.gov/pubs/GettingReadyCollegeEarly/index.html.

Wood, Terry. 1999. "Creating a Context for Argument in Mathematics Class." *Journal for Research in Mathematics Education* 30 (2): 171–91.

Index